THE RHETORICAL HERO

By the Same Author
LOGIC AND CRITICISM

THE RHETORICAL HERO

An Essay on the Aesthetics of André Malraux

by

WILLIAM RIGHTER

CHILMARK PRESS
New York

Printed in Great Britain

73242

Contents

Preface

There was an absolute of friendship for Malraux that a hundred posthumous judgements will be unable to blemish. There was a living Malraux, a weight of hot blood in the age's heart; there will be a dead Malraux, a prey to history.

—JEAN PAUL SARTRE, 1948.

ODDLY for a writer so involved with immediate situation as Sartre, specifically concerned at this point with 'writing for one's age', it is precisely the present tense that is here omitted. The 'hot blood in the age's heart' is implied to be a thing of the past, the 'prey to history' yet to come. Malraux seems uneasily suspended between a life which is over and a death which has not yet prepared him for the historical post-mortem. This curious lacuna clearly reflects the change in the situation of the writer between 1936 and 1948; it also reflects Sartre's uncertainty as to the nature of what has changed in Malraux. Between the vivid and committed reality of a former life and the remote perspective of historical time no viable image of Malraux comes ready to hand.

Since those words were written the career of Malraux has been full of content—his elaborate series of works on the psychology of art, the active political involvement as a Gaullist minister. Yet the character of his development has remained elusive—partly through the oblique relation of the new Malraux to the old, partly through the obscurity of the aesthetic writings themselves. This essay attempts a characterization of this last phase of Malraux's literary work, a philosophical interpretation of the aesthetic writings, and a tentative evaluation of

Malraux's *œuvre* in the light of them. I am of course quite aware that evaluation at this point may be far from complete, and that further works may alter our perspective. The bones of Malraux are far from ready for the definitive picking over. Yet I believe a distinctive pattern emerges from the work as a whole, and I have tried, among other things, to emphasize its continuity, to show the logic by which the essays on art have developed out of the novels, to define the interplay of art and action.

Translations of French passages are given at the foot of the page. As they are no more than a guide to the text I have tried to give the sense of a passage in its context, rather than a literal rendering or any approximation of Malraux's evocative style. I am grateful to Sheila Stern for her advice on the translations. To avoid a clutter of footnotes, references to Malraux's aesthetic writings have been put in parentheses in the text. A simple number gives the page reference to *Les Voix du Silence*, 1951, a number preceded by PA to *La Psychologie de l'Art* in the three volume Skira edition, Lausanne, 1949, or preceded by an S to *Saturne*, 1950, or by an M to *La Métamorphose des Dieux*, 1957. With the one exception they are all by Gallimard, Paris, and uniform in their editions. For kind permission to use the quoted material, including references to *Les Noyers de l'Altenburg* and the novels in the Pléiade Malraux, I am indebted to Editions Gallimard.

—Sa mythomanie est un moyen de nier la vie, n'est-ce pas,
de nier, et non pas d'oublier. Méfie-toi de la logique en ces
matières . . .

La Condition Humaine

I. The Evolution of an Aesthete

I. THE HISTORICAL MOMENT

IN a famous passage of 'The Intellectual Crisis' Valéry describes the anguish of the European 'Hamlet' of 1919. Torn between the claims of an archaic world order and the chaos that lies beyond it, oppressed by the weight of his traditions and his own incapacity to transcend them, he rummages among the splendid but unusable images of the past. In a parody of the graveyard scene he examines the skulls of the great creators, of Leonardo and Leibniz—much as the casual visitor may still examine the skull of Descartes, mounted and covered with minuscule handwriting as it sits among the freaks and fetishes of the Musée de L'Homme. The substance of this Hamlet's speculation is bones, the wreckage of the past, not the living flux of the world. His very problem might be described as what to call alive. In the confused aftermath of the great war so much seemed in ruin. And because his problem is the legacy of an historical event it presents itself to him quite naturally in historical terms. The dramatic posturing of this post-deluge Hamlet expresses an acute heightening of the historical sense, the realization that all civilization comes in the end to the ash-heap or the museum.

What Valéry's image fixes for us is the overriding obsession of an historical moment, with its consequent intensity of self-doubt. It is such an oppressive sense of historical crisis and painful self-consciousness in the face of it that forms the essential and primary context of the whole work of André Malraux, a context centred on the historical awareness of the destructibility of civilization and mankind. The actual working and relevance of such a primary context should become clear in the treating of particular works. The historical moment becomes intelligible through the details of its impact. But much in the interpretation of Malraux becomes plainer if this obsession is a recognized point of departure. It is in these terms that such oracular sayings as those about the 'death of man' or mankind's loss of credentials become immediately intelligible. They are straightforward comments on an historical situation. And I think it is inescapable to argue that a response to such an historical situation is as much the source of Malraux's aesthetic speculation as of his most engaged political novels.

Again it is in terms of such an historical moment that both the drama and contradictions of Malraux's career take on their meaning. Of course the novelty and glamour of his life of action has had the greatest share in creating Malraux's hold on the imagination. The ordinary novelist does not blow up the bridge himself while others hesitate, or receive General de Gaulle's accolade: 'Enfin, un homme!'[1] Certainly the sense of prodigy, the felt presence of a man wholly extraordinary and full of possibility had more to do with Malraux's immediate fame than did the qualities of the early books. From the beginning he was mythologized—eulogized as in Drieu la Rochelle's declamatory phrase: 'Malraux, homme nouveau, pose l'homme nouveau. L'homme éternel dans une de ses époques.'[2] Malraux's career begins in mystery with the expedition to Indo-China, the obscure affair of the missing statues, a short term of imprisonment, and a plunge into Eastern politics. The details of these matters are still unknown to us, but it is their resonance that counts. With all their shadow and uncertainty they nevertheless suggest a purity of adventure. Malraux entered the European consciousness, not as a writer but as an event, as a symbolic figure somehow combining the magical qualities of youth and heroism with a sense of unlimited promise. Here was no longer an air of defeat or fatigue, the melancholy self-deprecating

[1] Of course, much of the legend of Malraux is only doubtfully true. For a tentative effort to separate the man from the myth see W. M. Frohock, *Malraux and the Tragic Imagination*, Stanford, 1952.
[2] Pierre Drieu la Rochelle, *La Nouvelle Revue Française*, December, 1930. 'Malraux the new man reveals the new man. Eternal man in one of his epochs.'

'Hamlet' figure, but an insatiable cultural pirate, ransacking the four corners of the earth for some mysterious yet significant end, a last incarnation of 'Faustian man'.

Drieu's extravagant phrase reveals more about the needs of the time than about the subject that inspired it. Unlike the admiration one might normally feel for the heroes of the past, Drieu's response to Malraux is not concerned with the accomplishment of the man, but with the man himself as a form of natural historical evidence, an assurance, a breath of life. The action, the image, the quality of life—all predominate for Drieu over any real understanding of Malraux's purposes, or the interpretation of what he has written. 'La pensée de Malraux est fiévreuse, violente, obscure; mais son expérience est claire et ordonnée.'[1] The predominance may partly spring from an intellectual's delight in the simple purity of action. It may also express a gratitude for the fact of heroism without serious concern for its meaning. The great men of heroic ages are admired for their deeds, while the age itself is taken for granted; the life of Malraux suggests to his admirers that heroic ages are not altogether dead.

Such a symbolic existence, at a high level of self-consciousness, has complex responsibilities, above all the painful one of remaining true to itself. And no paradox of Malraux's career has more puzzled and inflamed both critics and admirers than the particular metamorphosis that has transformed the novelist of violence into a critic and curator, or the ardent revolutionary into a fixture of the established order. Accustomed to an image of restlessness and experiment, to a temperament committed to discovery and change, to the 'new man' himself, one feels uneasy in the presence of a conserver of political and intellectual traditions. The important changes here do not seem the ideological ones—although Malraux has had his sectarian critics, both Marxist and otherwise. The more genuine loss is the mythical being. The revolutionary spirit with its belief in the future, in the infinite plasticity and creativity of the human self seems to have fallen back on the ancient models, denying its extraordinary promise to relax into familiar and outworn forms. Such an alteration in Malraux seems the denial of change and invention,

[1] 'The thought of Malraux is feverish, violent, obscure; but his experience is clear and ordered.'

3

a denial possibly reflecting a decline of the creative powers of a great novelist, suggesting to some that the overwrought and pretentious essay has been substituted for real creation. The metamorphosis of Malraux would then testify to a double defeat, mythological and real—of a symbolic image of man and of an individual talent.

Nevertheless, such a cleanly antithetical picture of Malraux's development would be crude and misleading. It is clear that some kind of duality has existed from the start. The collector of art objects was present in the romantic explorer; the ambiguous relationship with the traditional past was given its first examination in Malraux's earliest important work, *La Tentation de l'Occident*. At this beginning point of his literary career Malraux felt the necessity of seeing human action in the clear light of reflection, and the role of the individual self in terms of a rationalized view of human history. The contrast of oriental and occidental minds is almost entirely devised to gain depth of perspective on the crisis of European culture. And even in the most turbulent of the early novels reflection exists in the midst of violence, an acute romantic self-consciousness in the moments of greatest abandon. The archaeologist joins with the adventurer and the smell of the lamp is mixed with the smell of battle. Malraux is from the beginning aware that history as creation and as action is never separable from that various spectacle that stretches backwards in time. In the same moment he plunges us forward into the flux of life—and yet points behind us to the assembled testimony of the past, to the library and the museum.

More than simply a duality of interest, all of Malraux's work presents an essential play between an action and its perspective, between the present and the eternal, between the loss of oneself in the moment and the recognition of oneself in terms of one's whole destiny. And this duality endures however violent the changes in ostensible subject matter or in genre. Or one might put it that the underlying subject matter itself never changes, and in his first works as in his last the same issues dominate: there is an obsessive and consistent investigation of the place of the private individual in historical time, the place of the individual passion in the overwhelming and unintelligible rush of events. And beyond the historical query lies a metaphysical one, distinguished not by its intellectual form but by its felt

4

presence and insistence, a dramatization of the human demand to know something of its place in the pattern of things beyond itself, to relate the very course of human history to some intelligible feature of the structure of things. In so far as Malraux can be called a philosophical novelist it is not on the grounds of theories he presents, but of philosophical queries which are dramatized by the lives of his characters, or later, analogous queries which other men have, however dimly, formulated in the world of art.

In the novels the model situation is that of the single individual faced by the extreme demands of the historical moment. Garine and Kyo, Hernandez, Manuel and Vincent Berger seek in such a moment to create through action, to alter the course of their world in a significant way. Their action is intended as revolt and as creation. But whatever the circumstances of the historical moment, something always challenges the meaning of both the action and its motives. The fact of cruelty or indifference, or of a particular death may put all human qualities in question. And in *Les Voix du Silence* this confrontation of human character by the facts of man's fate is universalized into the image of an historical apocalypse, of a day when no humanity will remain to observe or interpret the dead stones of Florence (638). Such an image is only an expansion or extension of what has gone before it, nothing of the substance, only the scale and form of Malraux's investigation has changed. What was implicit in the fictional situation is now generalized in discursive statement.

But the change from fiction to essay has not altogether deprived Malraux of the dramatic intensity of the novels. The tone of his aesthetic writings is that of a feverish conversation, interspersed with patches of reverie. Malraux is at once the dramatist of the world of art and the archaeologist of the human spirit. Not only is there a continuity of subject matter, but of feeling as well. For all the change in medium the attitude is astonishingly constant. Tchen's moment of suspense over the man he is to kill almost prefigures the impassioned spectator in the imaginary museum. Both are alone in the same reverie, confronted by the same question of 'What is man?', by the overpowering silence of those absolutes which Malraux sees as the essentials of the human situation: the incongruous facts of death and personal feeling, our crushing anonymity in the face of history and time. The two figures, the terrorist and the museum-goer, epitomize man's response to that situation, and it is their moment of illumination, this meditative interlude in the face of what is by all standards fundamental, that receives its full statement in *Les Voix du Silence*. Only in the end, the dramatic moment has become historical speculation.

It is important to say *historical* speculation because a close consideration of Malraux's aesthetic works shows less interest in art for its own sake than for what can be seen through it, or lies behind it. *Les Voix du Silence* contains no aesthetic theory of any novelty or importance, nor any argument of serious interest to the philosopher or critic of art. To compare it with other aesthetic philosophies that seek to analyse the character of art itself would be to misunderstand its purpose. For Malraux art is a vast reservoir of evidence, a means of demonstration, through which a series of queries and propositions about man's nature and history are unfolded. Kant said that of the four essential questions philosophy asks, 'What is man?' contains all the rest. To this question *Les Voix du Silence* sets out to give its oblique and figurative answer. Assuming that man's true nature is to be known through that which is most expressive and most permanent in his works, Malraux the curator has assembled from works of art a vast retrospective exhibition. The world of art is an elaborate testimonial to human creative power. The object of art itself becomes a link between the individual and history—an almost sacred meeting place of the self and the other.

2. THE NOVELS

The opaque surface of *Les Voix du Silence* seems designed to give away nothing about its origins, to appear as much as possible an apocalyptic breath from the void and to speak with a passionate directness from the immediate experience of the work of art in hand. That the background and development of his essential themes should only be seen obliquely is characteristic of Malraux. Yet a tracing, however fragmentary, of their evolution is important to the whole pattern of his work, whether connections are obscured by ellipsis or subordinated to the

6

demands of the immediate. There is some important pre-history, with specific intellectual debts which I shall consider in the next section. Here I want to look at the formulation of Malraux's 'philosophical' queries, and to outline their treatment in his novels.

Much lies in an inherited tradition of enquiry: the puzzled speculation before the image of man which is constant through Malraux's works has a venerable French ancestry. The re-formulation of the question 'What is man?' has been the obsession of French moralists and diarists from Montaigne to the present. And in Pascal ('Quel chimère est-ce donc que l'homme?') Malraux finds two of the key images which are to dominate his novels, those of the condemned man and of the *cachot*. These are instruments of the 'extreme situation' which ensure the profound isolation of a character from a normal human context, even separate him from the course of events which has produced his peril, an *arrachement* similar to that which is later applied to works of art. This 'literature of extreme situations' with its isolation of character for the individual moment of truth, frames itself quite easily in quasi-Cartesian terms—before the firing squad the old formula is twisted: 'I think, therefore I am, but in a moment . . . ' The political purposes, the individual passions, all the raison d'être of a personal situation vanish in the face of the elemental facts of life and death, and lives break off with a query which is neither answered nor entirely unanswered by death. 'Que l'histoire est peu de chose en face de la chair vivante—[in its last moment] encore vivante. . . '[1]

The force of Pascal's famous image lies in combining the psychological and the metaphysical:

> Qu'on s'imagine un nombre d'hommes en chaînes, et tous condamnés à la mort, dont les uns étant chaque jour égorgés à la vue des autres, ceux qui restent voient leur propre condition dans celle de leurs semblables, et se regardant les uns et les autres avec douleur et sans espérance, attendent à leur tour. C'est l'image de la condition des hommes.[2]

---

[1] *L' Espoir*, in *Romans*, Bibliothèque de la Pléiade, Paris, 1947, p. 650.
[2] *Pensées*—341 (Chevalier). 'Let one imagine a number of men in chains, and all condemned to death, some being each day executed in the sight of the others. Those who remain see their true state in that of their fellows, and look at one another in sorrow and without hope, awaiting their turn. That is the image of the human condition.'

Of this vignette the scene in the schoolyard in *La Condition Humaine* is of course the quite literal dramatization, as is the analogous scene in the prison yard at Toledo in *l'Espoir*. And the cachot,[1] mentioned so frequently in *l'Espoir* had its fullest use in *Le Temps de Mépris*. What is interesting in this is not only the derivation of the images, but the exact similarity of their use. The execution yard is an enclosed world, all of its inhabitants bound for a destination varied only by refinements in suffering, a medieval morality brought up to date. And in the cachot the human being is brought face to face not only with the possibilities of pain and death but with the limitations of his own endurance, the essential ideals and motives of his course of action, with their sustaining power or lack of it. Kassner in *Le Temps de Mépris* re-enacts the particulars of another phrase of Pascal, 'Is the sentence given? if so what and why?' Kassner is thrown back on his native human resources to preserve his sanity, and in total isolation must almost recreate himself through a combination of will and memory.

But for Pascal the extreme situation is more than a psychological device, it is the threshold of 'the wager'. In his metaphysical scheme it is all or nothing, the Kingdom or the void. N. Chiaramonte has remarked that Malraux wagers on the act as Pascal wagers on God.[2] But there is one overwhelming difference: to wager on God is in some way to understand or believe one understands the terms. The pure act is blind. Judged purely in terms of action the frenzied gesture may be worth the thoughtful construction. And this preoccupation with action that Chiaramonte has described so well may as easily refer to random energy, to forms of action undifferentiated even by the relative importance of their ends. The act exists in order to give meaning to human experience, and yet it is an arbitrary meaning; in most cases its validity derives not from the fact of the action but from certain qualities of the actor himself. The act, for Malraux, in effect has meaning in so far as it is *expressive* of some essential element of our humanity—even perhaps, in so far as it has *style*. The act, therefore, depends, even in the earliest novels, on values that are to some extent aesthetic. It is expres-

---

[1] *Pensées*—342.
[2] Nicola Chiaramonte, 'Malraux and the Demons of Action', *Partisan Review*, Vol. XV.

siveness that gives dignity, or pathos or power. The result is to place achievement, purpose, the social and human consequences of action, however much they may have dominated the narrative, finally subordinate to the human qualities discovered by the way. Great undertakings are less important in what they accomplish for us than for what they reveal in us.

On the whole, the action of Malraux's heroes accomplishes little: revolutions fail, projects are abandoned, no course of affairs seems to work towards any decisive conclusion. Rather it is the style of the man, the unique human quality displayed that is of ultimate value. (And along with the romantic figures, Clappique too has his style, as much or more than the heroic protagonists, and his hold on the imagination is as great as any of theirs.)[1] Certainly scenes are designed with this stylized heightening of all of their expressive elements in the foreground. The tender fraternal embrace at the end of *Les Conquérants*, the rhetorical flourish that concludes *La Voie Royale* could only have been conceived with their theatrical and gestural qualities essential to their meaning. And some of the greatest scenes of *La Condition Humaine*, the interview in Koenig's office, or Ferral's release of the birds, are so purely gesture that the theatrical quality exists for its own sake.

Consequently, two elements seem to work side by side: the concentration on episodes involving the psychological moment of truth, and the selection of those stylized and expressive features of human behaviour that are intrinsically dramatic and psychologically revealing. Added to an extraordinary sense of movement they produce the often noticed 'cinematographic' quality of Malraux's novels—'cinematographic' in the sense of moving from image to image, rather than from event to event —where it is the flow of images that controls the narrative. But even if deprived of that sense of movement the individual fragments exist as 'stills' and are perhaps more interesting as isolated images: in a way Malraux's technique is better described as the careful arrangement of psychological snapshots, a curious forerunner of the Imaginary Museum where the same critical faculty is at work isolating and framing the expressive and revealing artistic gesture. To such a sensibility the use of aesthetic criteria in the judgment of human action is perfectly natural.

[1] Cf. Frohock, op. cit., Appendix.

In some cases the aesthetic sense penetrates the 'extreme situation' itself. Where bravado or self-pity before pain, torture or the firing squad would be in bad taste, aesthetically inappropriate, a fatalistic stoicism is not. This is, of course, an attitude which Malraux shares with several contemporaries, above all with Hemingway for whom war or the bullfight produces a similar mixture of aesthetic standards and 'extreme situation'. Indifference to danger and death is the mark of the hero, and achieves its drama of understatement when death is most certain, most vividly in the case of Katov in *La Condition Humaine* who, led off to die in the fire box of a locomotive, mutters to himself 'Allons, supposons que je sois mort dans un incendie'.

But however strong the emphasis in the early novels on stoicism, balance, aesthetic detachment, Malraux's treatment of his characters is seldom cool and reflective. The heroic actors carry the narrative by sheer élan: Perken in *La Voie Royale* somehow succeeds in accepting the swift inevitability of his death and yet maintains the inflexible will, devoted in its demise to its original dream. For both Perken and Garine it is the defeat of the will that is the significant part of their story; their defence against an individual fate is a violent and unintelligible struggle. But however close this may come to a tragic model one is hardly purged through pity and fear. The total effect is rather a chaos of romantic excitement, a murky evocation of some spiritual triumph in actual defeat, where the glory of human powers is exalted over the circumstances of their fall. In the three major novels through *La Condition Humaine* it is the sense of triumph in defeat that seems meant to linger in the mind. Only in *L'Espoir* is a more collective humanity bolstered at the end by an official victory. Of all of the novels this is the least romantic, and least deeply involved in the intensities of personal drama. The will of the individual is eclipsed by the common struggle, as if some glittering dimension of humanity had been eroded by the attrition of war. The characters are less forcefully and individually present (if sometimes more solidly), and carry less of our personal concern with them. The death of Hernandez is not the climactic event of a personal drama, but an episode in that common struggle in which all humanity is absorbed. So the emphasis lies precisely on that feeling of common humanity, on what we share with others rather than what marks off the hero from the common run of mankind, a sense of the human community which is repeated in the opening pages of *Les Noyers de l'Altenburg*.

It is in this last of Malraux's published novels that the persistent themes of the earlier ones are essentially altered; however, the alteration is not of substance but of perspective and of treatment. For in a way *Les Noyers de l'Altenburg* is a compendium of earlier materials: the prison scenes, the point of death in battle, the exotic journeys, the moments of heroic or of vain and destructive action—but all give place to the demands of reflective intelligence. The model situations are re-enacted from the point of view of the detached observer, and the important events are the reflections, or particular perceptions of the mind. War in the desert, or in the trenches, or with the tanks is the *mise en scène* for a discussion of causes and consequences, and becomes the subject matter of reflection. The vision of the walnut trees or of the faces in the camp at Chartres suggests general conclusions and philosophical theories about the continuity of man, and about those durable features of his character that underlie all human history. The imprisoned narrator is wholly different from his predecessor Kassner. Kassner in his prison cell maintains his humanity as an act of endurance. The narrator of *Les Noyers de l'Altenburg* is essentially an observer whose own humanity and fate are not central issues. To him 'humanity' is an object and puzzle for the understanding, alternatively a brute presence, or an historical abstraction, or simply the eternal model for an object of art. In the lives of both of the Bergers one moves from heated action to detached reflection; but the essential issues are not so much dramatized as debated. The trial imposed by events is only the prelude to an effort of the understanding, the attempt to see the consequences of action in terms of an intelligible view of man and his history. In comparing observations and episodes, in probing for the significance of their 'encounters with man', their intelligence always reaches for general and historical explanations, and the proper setting for such a form of enquiry is the library or in the talk of the intellectuals gathered in the priory at Altenburg.

Hovering as it does between fiction and essay *Les Noyers de l'Altenburg* is perhaps unsatisfactory as an artistic whole. It is episodic, loosely constructed, with fragments of action separated by long passages of intellectual talk, and the point of view in the intellectual enquiry uncertainly divided between father and son. Yet there is a clear pattern established in the succession of three generations, and the experiences of father and son have a precise symmetry. Their 'encounters with man' occur in crises which are not personal but those of civilization itself. Through the demolition of the two great wars they are forced to reassess their knowledge of man. Malraux situates his work in the moment of defeat, when the collapse of France seemed like the collapse of civilization itself. In turning to examine that collapse and its consequences *Les Noyers de l'Altenburg* represents an important break in his thought and a return to his earlier attempt to diagnose the maladies of our civilization in *La Tentation de l'Occident*: the two world crises are parallel, and are occasions for similar investigations.

In *La Tentation de l'Occident* of 1926 both the content and the manner of later work is suggested. The Malraux who asks in 1948 if the death of man is not the central problem of our civilization has already phrased the same query in his youth:

> La réalité absolue a été pour vous [European man] Dieu, puis l'homme; mais *l'homme est mort*, après Dieu, et vous cherchez avec angoisse celui à qui vous pourriez confier son étrange héritage.[1]

This short essay, consisting of the imaginary correspondence of a young Frenchman travelling in the Orient and a young Chinese travelling in Europe, is an attack on the cultural self-sufficiency of a Europe which, as for Valéry's Hamlet, has lost the possibility of belief in its own destiny. The letters of the European are romantic and groping, reaching from his own discontent towards values which the Orient dimly suggests. Those of the Chinese are cold and sceptical, incisive reflections on an inadequate world order. The argument of both is that the possibilities of western man are exhausted, and that this 'death' is felt in the European soul. After the death of God, the victim of nineteenth-century science, comes the 'death' of man, the victim of his own passion for destruction, leaving for the future as Malraux elsewhere says, nothing beyond the 'nihilistic will'.

---

[1] *La Tentation de l'Occident*, Paris, 1926, pp. 174–5. 'Absolute reality was for you God, and then man; but man is dead after God, and you search in anguish for someone to whom you can entrust his strange heritage.'

After almost twenty years and in the face of renewed crisis *Les Noyers de l'Altenburg* sets out to re-analyse this loss of faith and to relate it more specifically to the details of individual experience and historical circumstance. While its more romantic episodes revive the glittering image of the man of action, these remain marginal to the central issues of the book. The heroic career of Berger senior is only a backdrop for the conversations at Altenburg, and serves largely to create the proper status for his rôle in the intellectual debate. His past as a man of action gives his word a special force, but this is action 'recollected in tranquillity'. Whatever qualities his character may have displayed in the moments of 'extreme situation' are barely sketched as the prolegomenon to talk. Throughout the novel characterization is minimal; we recognize few individual contours of either father or son. Those devices and atmospheric touches that suggest the earlier novels have lost their dramatic movement, and the fragmentary, unrealized quality of the episodes is surely intentional. These are only selected events, analogous to case studies perhaps, which bear on the novel's central theme of the disintegration of the image of man.

The true context of the action is history itself. Here again, another form of *arrachement* is practised, wholly different from that of the *cachot*. For it is not the relation of a personal crisis to its human context that is destroyed here, but the sense of historical context itself. The personal existence of the single man is no longer on trial, but the historical existence and *raison d'être* of the abstraction 'man'. The moments of violence, often brilliant in themselves, have their validity now as an uncertain evidence of a more general kind—they come now not between one man and his world, but between all men and the very possibility of a world. The unhappy microcosm of the tank has a double isolation, within and without. Corresponding to the breakdown of mechanical communication within is the detachment from the natural dimensions that normally frame the human world:

> Du vieil accord de l'homme et de la terre, il ne reste rien: ces blés où nous tanguons dans l'obscurité ne sont plus des blés, mais des camouflages . . .[1]

[1] *Les Noyers de l'Altenburg*, Paris, 1948, p. 269. 'Of the old accord between man and the earth nothing remains; these wheatfields where we pitch and roll in the darkness are no longer fields but camouflages.'

Tanks and camouflage are the devices of men, and as a result of human invention the 'old accord' has been broken . . . only perhaps to be restored in humiliation and defeat, in the stunned recognition of one's natural humanity in the camp at Chartres.

The novelist's interest here is not in the psyche under stress, or even in the personal psychology of defeat. His aim is rather to seek general explanations, to create a framework in which experience becomes intelligible, and in *Les Noyers de l'Altenburg* this framework is a mixture of the historical and metaphysical, or perhaps the historical raised to some curious metaphysical status. 'C'est l'histoire qui est chargée de donner un sens à l'aventure humaine—comme les dieux. De relier l'homme à l'infini.'[1] History is given the task of ultimate explanations, and although this remark comes from the sceptic Mollberg as the preface to a denial ('car l'homme est un hasard, et, pour l'essentiel, le monde est fait d'oubli.')[2] it is still the shared assumption of all of the speakers at the Altenburg colloquium that any understanding of the final character and destiny of mankind is to be found in the study of the human past. The facts of the human condition, the quality and uniqueness of the human record are the only possible evidence which can bear upon that 'sense' to the human adventure. But what can such an enquiry tell us about the connection of man and the 'infinite?' In groping with this elusive matter Malraux's colloquists exploit three lines: a conceptual investigation into the meaning of the notion 'man', an historical investigation into the meaning of the 'evidence' drawn from the human past, and finally an irrational response to the contradictions of argument that is best described as 'visionary'.

None of these elements gets an exclusive or coherent treatment; methods of discourse are constantly mingled in the unsteady flow of conversation. The conflicting voices suggest the unresolved state of mind of the narrator—the whole mélange a representation of the intellectual conflict within Malraux himself. But however intellectually the problems may be framed, or however flat and academic the quality of the talk at Altenburg, the arguments are still subordinated to a dramatic pattern

[1] p. 140. 'It is history that is charged with giving sense to the human adventure —like the gods. To connect man with the infinite.'

[2] p. 142. ' . . . for man is an accident, and essentially, the world consists of oblivion.'

in which the visionary elements have both the first and the last word. The shadow of Nietzsche is heavy on this work, as it is in one degree or another over the whole of Malraux, and an anecdote of Nietzsche's madness prefaces the colloquium and lends it something of an apocalyptic tone. It also serves to define the colloquium's essential as opposed to its formal subject: 'Man against nothingness' is the issue that peers out through 'The Permanence and Metamorphosis of Man'.

The narrator's uncle, the patron of Altenburg, was charged with bringing Nietzsche from Turin to Basle after his final breakdown. In the long darkness of the train journey through the St. Gotthard tunnel:

> ... une voix commençà de s'élever dans le noir, au-dessus du tintamarre des essieux. Friedrich chantait—avec une articulation parfaite, lui qui, dans la conversation, bredouillait—il chantait un poème inconnu à nous; et c'etait son dernier poème, Venise. Je n'aime guère la musique de Friedrich. Elle est médiocre. Mais ce chant était ... eh bien, mon Dieu: sublime.[1]

The third-class railway carriage, with its peasant woman and her chicken, some workers, a dentist, becomes a microcosm, the journey symbolic:

> C'était la vie—je dis simplement: la vie ... Il se passait un ... événement très singulier: le chant était aussi fort qu'elle. Je venais de découvrir quelque chose. Quelque chose d'important. Dans la prison dont parle Pascal, les hommes sont parvenus à tirer d'eux-mêmes une réponse qui envahit, si j'ose dire, d'immortalité, ceux qui en sont dignes. ...
>
> Et dans ce wagon, voyez-vous, et quelquefois ensuite—je dis seulement: quelquefois ... —les millénaires du ciel étoilé m'ont semblé aussi effacés par l'homme, que nos pauvres destins sont effacés par le ciel étoilé. ...[2]

[1] p. 96. ' ... a voice began to arise in the darkness, above the clattering of the wheels. Frederich was singing—with perfect articulation, he who in conversation stuttered and stumbled—he sang a poem unknown to us; it was his last poem, 'Venice'. I do not care much for the music of Friedrich. It is mediocre. But this song was ... well, my God, sublime.'

[2] p. 97. 'It was life—I say simply: life ... Then occurred a very singular event. The song had a force equal to life itself. I discovered something, something important. In the prison of which Pascal speaks, men succeed in drawing from themselves a response which floods, if I may put it so, with immortality, those who are worthy of it.
And in that railway carriage, you see, and sometimes afterwards ... I say only sometimes ... the infinitudes of the starry sky have seemed as much effaced by man, as our poor destinies are effaced by the starry sky ... '

Allowing for a touch of spiritual inflation in all of the remarks of the narrator's uncle, the episode acts both as a frame to much of what follows, and puts in relief some essential questions. We are faced at once with the problems of '. . . ceux qui en sont dignes . . . ' of immortality, a question which is inseparable for Malraux from any attempt to postulate a solution to his obsessive enquiry into the *meaning of the notion of man*. In the case of Nietzsche it is genius, even in madness, which has challenged the nothingness with a visionary response. Genius in the form of a poet's commentary has suggested that what lies within man matters as much as what lies without: 'Le plus grand mystère n'est pas que nous soyons jetés au hasard entre la profusion de la matière et celle des astres; c'est que, dans cette prison, nous tirions de nous-mêmes des images assez puissantes pour nier notre néant.'[1] The drawing of images from himself, with its overtones of creation ex-nihilo, focuses quite naturally on the figure of the artist. The case of the artist will recur throughout the discussion at Altenburg, and the anecdote about Nietzsche is as much an oblique introduction to the symposium on 'The Eternal Elements of Art' which does not take place, as it is to that on 'the Permanence and Metamorphosis of Man' which does. And the moral of the Nietzsche episode is at once enforced by one drawn from the visual arts, '. . . vous . . . connaissez la tête de jeune homme du musée de l'Acropole? La première sculpture qui ait représenté un visage humain, simplement un visage humain; libéré des monstres . . . de la mort . . . des dieux. Ce jour-là, l'homme aussi a tiré l'homme d'argile . . .'[2]

For the moment the artist remains a point of reference to which the imagination frequently returns, but which exists on the periphery of the main discussion. The assembled philosophers, artists and scientists concerned with the 'Permanence and Metamorphosis of Man' are primarily involved with the challenge of the celebrated anthropologist Mollberg whose intervention gives the conversations much of their overwrought intensity and dramatic conflict. Although Malraux may have

[1] pp. 98-99. 'The greatest mystery is not that we are thrown by chance between the profusion of matter and the stars; it is that, in this prison, we draw images from ourselves powerful enough to deny our nothingness.'

[2] p. 98. '. . . you . . . do you know the head of a young man from the Acropolis museum? The first sculpture which represented a human face, simply a human face; freed from monsters . . . from death . . . from the gods. On that day, man also created man from clay . . .'

16

abandoned the drama of violent action for the medium of talk, the impact of words may still be more in their force than in their sense. The dramatic elements of this conflict weigh more than the intellectual ones. Having scattered the pages of his unfinished masterpiece on 'Civilization as Conquest and Destiny' on the African sands, Mollberg proposes that the evidence, drawn from the whole range of human knowledge, leads us to the conclusion that man's destiny can have no meaning, because the very notion of 'Man' has in itself no proper boundaries or essential sense. The plunge into the past reveals man as indistinguishable from his natural context, and for the most part incapable of so distinguishing himself. The efforts of the more advanced civilizations to do so are a form of self-inflation which would be the more foolish if it were not tragic.

Two kinds of argument enter into this. One is the evidence drawn from primitive peoples of their incapacity to distinguish themselves from the animals with whom their lives are spent. The other is less empirical if quite conventionally scientific: disguised by language and ritual our behaviour re-enacts a pattern common to the whole organic world, and such behaviour is in no significant sense specifically 'human'. This of course is an argument which depends on the persuasive use of its key terms: Mollberg proposes a purely nominalistic use of the word 'man' making it a simple classification which has neither biological nor metaphysical importance. And the ground for this is for the most part ignored. An interlocutor who observes that man may well be part of the natural order, but unique in certain properties quite worth discussing, is not refuted but swept away by the tide of nihilism. Mollberg's argument, with its mixture of positivist commonplace and romantic allusion (which may owe something to its model in Leo Frobenius) is designed to overwhelm rather than to convince. Mollberg himself is the 'nihilistic will' in scientific dress. He proposes a ground for the felt dilemma of the colloquium, that the notion of man has been eroded by science and history. His is the *coup de grâce* delivered to hearers already heavy with a sense of historical fatalism, already obsessed by the twilight of their culture.

The discourse of Mollberg is not only obscure, but is at moments handled with an ironical touch. Malraux seems aware how easily such talk is dominated by charlatanism and self-importance. But the emotional aftermath is real enough, and the fear that man is no more than a straw in the wind, that civilization is an insignificant and perishable veneer, produces an atmosphere of 'panic and emptiness' rather than an intellectual challenge. The confrontation is rather with a vague and threatening series of possibilities, where the mortality of civilization and meaninglessness of that individual thing, man, loom out of shadowy uncertainty. It is probably an appropriate part of the novelist's licence that he should frame his situation in this way, and that each character should respond individually to Mollberg's nihilism according to the qualities of a particular and personal *Angst*. The intellectual uncertainties surely reflect the extent to which *Les Noyers de l'Altenburg* is a tentative work, something of a trial run. But the stutterings and misgivings which follow Mollberg's discourse are also meant to indicate the force of the nihilistic vision he has let loose.

Certainly the response to it is not put in argument, but in so far as it has a positive character is entirely visionary. For Vincent Berger before the Gothic library or above all in his moment of flight from the futility of speech among the trees of the walnut grove that surround the library of Altenburg, there is a sudden and overwhelming sense of the human identity: the walnut carved into Gothic faces lining the library walls is wholly different from the natural profusion of the grove itself. In the capacity to create form the fact of man's presence and powers seems once more meaningful. And this capacity conjoins with that suggested by one of Mollberg's interlocutors, that the significant and perhaps divine element of man is precisely his power to 'put the world in question'. The fact of man in the universe is the fact of a commentary, the capacity to respond—whether through words or forms. To question, to arraign the natural order of things, is itself a unique event in that natural order.

Already, in *Les Noyers de l'Altenburg*, visual art is for Malraux the most congenial and suggestive form of this power; more even than speculative thought it is man's attempt to reconstruct the world on a scale more his own:

> Notre art me paraît une rectification du monde, un moyen d'échapper à la condition d'homme. La confusion capitale me paraît venir de ce qu'on a cru—dans l'idée que nous faisons de la

tragédie grecque c'est éclatant—que représenter une fatalité
était la subir. Mais non! c'est presque la posséder. Le seul fait de
pouvoir la représenter, de la concevoir, la fait échapper au vrai
destin, à l'implacable échelle divine; la réduit à l'échelle humaine.
Dans ce qu'il a d'essentiel, notre art est une humanisation du
monde.[1]

Here, in rather fragmentary miniature, the argument of *Les
Voix du Silence* is compressed: the artist's action is not a simple
representation but a taking possession and transformation, a
re-ordering of the world which fixes the place and power of the
human presence in it. However, this suggestion is largely abandoned in the conversations that follow, and only momentarily
re-affirmed by the vision among the walnut trees. What is lacking
is any attempt to estimate the consequences of the artist's act, to
draw any detailed conclusions about what is demonstrated
through works of art, or to show what the particular characters
of the great styles assert about the human presence. But the
most characteristic quality of the artist's action is defined in the
contrast between 'submission' and 'possession'. Most men submit to their fate, accept it as the normal course of human life.
Through his attempt to represent this fatality the artist challenges it; his creativity devises another world, a counter-world
so to speak, and such creation is an act of possession, at once a
rectification and humanization of the original. 'Qu'est-ce que
l'acanthe grecque? Un artichaut stylisé. Stylisé, c'est-à-dire
humanisé: tel que l'homme l'eût fait s'il eût été Dieu.'[2] And the
same argument is repeated in *Les Voix du Silence:* 'Tout artichaut
porte en lui une feuille d'acanthe, et l'acanthe est ce que
l'homme eût fait de l'artichaut si Dieu lui eût demandé conseil'
(74).[3]

The great interest of *Les Noyers de l'Altenburg* does not lie
in its intrinsic qualities as a work of art, but in its detailed

[1] p. 128. 'Our art seems to me a rectification of the world, a means of escape from
the human condition. The great confusion seems to me to come from one's having
believed—in the idea we have of Greek tragedy it is striking—that to represent a
fatality was to submit to it. But no! it is almost to possess it. The simple power of
representing it, of conceiving it, enables it to escape true destiny, from the implacable divine scale; reduces it to the human scale. In so far as it touches the essential, our art is a humanization of the world.'
[2] p. 127–8. 'What is a Greek acanthus? A stylized artichoke. Stylized, that is to
say, humanized: such as man would have made if he had been God.'
[3] 'Every artichoke carries in itself an acanthus leaf, and the acanthus is what man
would have made of the artichoke if God had asked his counsel.'

indications of a stage in Malraux's development. It reveals the continuity of his themes, and the effects of a re-assessment are shown through his altered attitude towards them. That his romantic imagination is as much at home in historical speculation as in dramatizing the moment of crisis should be expected —Malraux had begun in this manner in *La Tentation de l'Occident*. But both tone and direction of the speculation have changed enormously. The earlier work is concerned with a liberation from European parochialism, with the rejection of western values that seemed moribund. *Les Noyers de l'Altenburg* shows a complete reversal; Malraux has turned back to a traditional western culture; his images are drawn from the Gothic priory, from Chartres, from Nietzsche and Pascal. If these latter might once have been the instruments of challenge, they have here become the established features of a traditional culture. And through the reflections of the two Bergers runs their strong sense of family tradition. The wheel seems to have come full circle, with the surrealist and revolutionary returned to a tradition that is very much his own, and the novel becomes a moving tribute to the 'old Europe' faced by another deluge. Yet the return is not to Europe alone. In the experience of the two Bergers remote civilizations have been assimilated and made familiar. The whole tradition of human culture, in all of its variety, has captured Malraux's imagination, and behind this passionate desire to somehow see humanity whole lies the pressure, so persistent in *Les Noyers de l'Altenburg*, to assert the continuity and 'permanence' of man.

This obsession seems an intellectual curiosity in itself, although psychologically intelligible, and true to its dramatic position in a novel concerned with crisis and defeat, with the possible collapse of the European order. But this atmosphere owes its urgency to more than an immediate historical crisis, and to the doctrines of a more famous prophet than Leo Frobenius. Part of the obscurity of Mollberg's discourse may be due to its mixing of two kinds of argument, drawn from quite different sources, from the reductivist and anti-humanist anthropological doctrines of Frobenius himself, and from the well-known denial of the continuity of civilization in the historical fatalism of Oswald Spengler. Here again is both an intellectual and a dramatic model.

3. ANTECEDENTS

The impact and imaginative power of Spengler's *Decline of the West* is easily forgotten in its present disrepute. For a generation that looked on the great war as the death agony of civilization, and which sought in history both analogues and explanations, Spengler often seemed gifted with prophecy. With a manner that mixed scientific and vatic assurance he delineated the natural course of the dying culture, and related it to its model in the disintegration of the ageing organism. Certainly the impression on Malraux was enormous, partly perhaps because of Spengler's capacity for combining prophetic intensity with a profusion of historical detail. Malraux has been quoted as saying that the primary intellectual task of his generation was the refutation of Spengler. In retrospect the problem seems neither intellectual, nor precisely one of refutation. The strength of Spengler is hardly in argument and his logical vulnerability is notorious. It is as the dramatic interpreter of crisis that he interests us. He more than any other philosopher of history is immersed in the historical moment in spite of his avowed wish to stand aloof in the abstraction of general laws, and his fatalistic tone was perfectly adapted to the mood of that young European whom Malraux has described: 'Lacking a doctrine [he] has nothing left but the will to give battle. And of that will nothing is left but weakness and fear. Our epoch . . . does not reveal the core of its thought, which is nihilistic, destructive, fundamentally negative.'[1]

Nor does Malraux anywhere attempt a 'refutation' by means of argument, or concern himself with any of the logical problems of Spengler's theory, He in fact nowhere displays any taste for disputation, or critical analysis, or the dissection of argument. Of his rather few critical essays none is designed to demolish, but all are appreciations, laying bare the unique or exciting elements of a particular intelligence or sensibility. Like most of his observations about individual paintings his critical reflections—say on the two Lawrences, or Faulkner—are penetrating acts of sympathy, always reaching for the unique contours of individual genius.

Malraux may well believe that destructive analytic criticism

[1] In Chiaramonte, op. cit.

is an irrelevant procedure, and might hold that if we demolished all of Spengler's arguments yet the substance could still be true. Clearly, the 'refutation' required is something of a different order, and can mean to Malraux nothing less than the provision of a wholly convincing alternative. He sees his own task as inventive or creative, directed to the construction of an opposing and equally synoptic image of human culture, and presenting it with the utmost persuasive power. So the point of contact with his adversary is only implicit, but nonetheless real. All the 'testimony' of Les Voix du Silence denies the Spenglerian proposition that cultures grow old and die in a life cycle as exigent as that of the natural world. The passion for continuity has produced (or rather adapted) its own conceptual invention, and the notion of 'metamorphosis' has come to rescue civilization from biological fatalism.

However, there is an involvement with Spengler that goes beyond this immediate level of 'challenge and response'. Far from the first to devise a cyclical theory of history, Spengler was perhaps the first to support it with evidence drawn from the whole range of human activity, from science and mathematics, literature and art. (Although in the use of literary evidence he has a predecessor in Vico.) While his feeling for the visual arts was relatively slight, his feeling for music—the most time bound of all the arts—was intense and profound. In the varieties of musical forms, as with those of architecture and mathematics, he found a rich supply of analogues, of patterns of growth, development and decline, that somehow measured the inner structure of a civilization's soul, forms that supplied the significant clue to reveal the whole. Underlying the particular forms and most revealing of all is that subtle yet abstractable quality common to all human creation, *style*. His remark that 'The task before art history is to write the comparative biography of the great styles'[1] could be taken as one of the prescriptions which Malraux's aesthetic works are meant to fulfil —however different their ultimate version of what the 'great styles' may say.

The belief that somehow a work of art is a skeleton key opening the dark recesses of a civilization is a legacy of romanticism and the expression theory of art. It is of course impossible

[1] Oswald Spengler, *The Decline of the West*, New York, 1928, I, p. 206.

to say how far Malraux has followed the specific suggestions of Spengler, and how far they have common ancestors in German romanticism and aesthetic theory—above all in Nietzsche. But there are remarkable resemblances between them, some in a shared sense of apocalyptic atmosphere, others in particular borrowings or turns of phrase. Spengler speaks in the same manner of the 'stock of forms that possesses duration', which becomes for Malraux a substratum of forms awaiting metamorphosis. And both speak of a durable and serious language of forms emancipated from the mundane and evanescent functions of ordinary language. In Spengler's notion of 'ornament' we have suggested Malraux's drama of the confrontation of the world by its art: ornament does not follow the natural order of life, but faces it.

These aesthetic terms, above all the notion of a 'language of forms', have an elaborate history. Speaking of the obscurity of the origins of *Les Voix du Silence* Pierre de Boisdeffre mentions ' . . . des emprunts, trop souvent passés sous silence, aux esthéticiens allemands, ou à des contemporains comme Élie Faure . . .'[1] None of the borrowings is actually detailed, and the reference is perhaps to a whole climate of opinion rather than to specific debts—although the evocative manner of speaking of 'forms' as independent spiritual entities following a mysterious course of their own is shared in Malraux and Faure's *Esprit des Formes*. But there is a more direct and powerful influence in Henri Focillon, especially in *La Vie des Formes* where certain specific concepts of *Les Voix du Silence* have at least a preliminary development. This is particularly true of Malraux's own use of the concept of 'style', of the notion, so important in *Les Voix du Silence* of a 'metamorphosis of forms', and there is even a hint of the idea of the *Imaginary Museum*.

In the case of 'style', there is much that could indicate a common origin, or at least a way of speaking shared widely among contemporaries. This could include the analogies of 'style' to language: speaking of 'vocabulary' and 'syntax', also the talk of its 'inner logic' and 'dialectic'. But two remarks are directly suggestive of Malraux's most important themes. Focillon

---

[1] Pierre de Boisdeffre, *André Malraux*, Paris, 1959, p. 94. ' . . . some borrowings, too often passed over in silence, from German aestheticians, or from such contemporaries as Élie Faure. . . . '

speaks of the word 'style' as indicating a special and superior quality in works of art, above all '... the eternal value, that allows it to escape the bondage of time'. And the notion is extended and applied to the very puzzle of the Altenburg colloquium: 'One style comes to an end; another comes to life. It is only natural that mankind should revaluate these styles over and over again, and it is in the application of this task that I apprehend the constancy and identity of the human spirit.' This notion of continuity is in turn directly connected with the concept of 'metamorphosis': 'Plastic forms are subjected to the principle of metamorphoses, by which they are perpetually renewed ...' and '... primarily form is a mobile life in a changing world. Its metamorphoses endlessly begin anew, and it is by the principle of style that they are above all coordinated and stabilized'. Finally, in attempting a redefinition of the doctrine of artistic influence Focillon foreshadows the special connection of works within the Imaginary Museum. The individual artist is not only contemporary with his generation, but with 'the spiritual group of which he is a member ... Herein lies the explanation of the rôle of museums in the nineteenth century: they assisted the various families of the mind in their work of self definition and union, beyond all demands of place or time'. And of the special relation of works within the museum 'Between masters who have never had the slightest personal acquaintance, and whom everything had kept apart—nature, distance, time —the life of forms establishes an intimate relationship.'[1]

I do not know how much importance should be given to such correspondences. For one thing, Malraux gives little in the way of direct clues to his reading. Is his notion of the autonomy of art indebted to Riegl? or to its ultimate Hegelian source?[2] Are there specific debts to Wörringer? or to Faure? Something may be accounted for by the fact that a number of these doctrines relating expression to form, forms to civilizations, and forms to other forms, were 'in the air'. In any case, connections are purely hypothetical. I have mentioned Focillon because resemblances seemed apparent, and because his work was published

[1] Henri Focillon, *The Life of Forms*, New York, 1948, pp. 4–12, 62–4.
[2] See E. Wind, *Art and Anarchy*, London, 1963, Chapter I, on the Hegelian origins of the notion of the autonomy of art and its consequences. And p. 129, a note on the impact of Riegl's doctrine.

in the middle 1930's, at approximately the moment acknowledged as the point at which Malraux began his aesthetic works (1935). But the question of actual influences is hardly important, and whatever voices were in the air acted to give both impetus and shape to Malraux's lifelong interest in art, and perhaps reinforced the conviction that the visual arts were the appropriate medium through which to work out the historical theses so long implicit in his work. Whether German or French aestheticians, whether Frobenius or Spengler, Nietzsche or Hegel, such influences were obviously tools ready to hand, subordinated to an imagination and a will that have assimilated and transformed them in a wholly personal creation.

Malraux and his predecessors share two notions which are profoundly conjoined. One is the view of 'style' as being the most important means through which the expressive powers of art work; the other is of the subordination of 'speaking', that is of ordinary conceptual thought, to the deeper revelation obtained through the mysterious logic through which a style unfolds itself. 'It's not the style, but the stuff, that stupefies'—to invert a mnemonic slogan. And Malraux has from the start been excited by the obscure world of evocation lying behind the great works: Claude says in *La Voie Royale*, 'What interests me most in works of art is their deeper life, the life made up of the deaths of men.'

Certain aestheticians believe that the symbolic-expressive element takes precedence over the communicative function of language—and language itself is only a small part of the vast human repertoire of expressive devices, from scowls and gestures to the great masterpieces themselves.[1] In Spengler a passionate anti-rationalism degrades even further the communicative value of speech; his noblest model of the understanding is that of the aged peasants whose best form of speech is silence, who have that deep sense of communion which reaches far below the conceptual surface that ordinary speech employs. Perhaps this image of such a depth of rapport helped suggest the peasant couple in the final scene of *Les Noyers de l'Altenburg*, who sit calmly through the warfare around them because there is

[1] Cassirer, Langer, etc., see S. Langer, *Philosophy in a New Key*, London, 1951, Chapter V.

nothing else to do. But it can hardly be intended as an image of subrational man—rather of man's persistence, a testimonial to the toughness of that old Europe that through whatever cataclysm refuses to die. In waiting to 'just wear out' it has outlived and will outlive the violence and chaos around it. Yet Malraux's peasants also suggest that when one looks to the fundamental one looks beyond talk, above all beyond the thin academic talk in the priory at Altenburg. Whether one looks to the simple facts of the human condition, or to the great masterpieces that tap the underground stream, whatever is essential speaks with the voices of silence.

4. FROM IMAGE TO 'ARGUMENT'

A formula for Malraux's response to the nihilistic antihumanism and historical fatalism of Mollberg's 'line' could be an overly neat reaffirmation of his belief in man's cultural heritage, and an historical testimonial to the continuity of human creative powers, in effect a conventional conservative pointing to the approved elements of the past. Yet *Les Voix du Silence* is a testimonial of a curious kind. Behind its nervous energy there is a passionate denial that affirmation or acceptance involves passive conformity; and its heightened, contorted style seems as determined to remake on its own ground the image of the culture it records, as to make the awareness of traditional culture somehow revolutionary. There is nothing in it of conventional art history, any more than of aesthetic theory—and Malraux behaves as if he wished by his own imaginative and rhetorical power to alter the nature of his material, to create the substance with the style, a subject matter *ex machina*. Historical facts are not brought to the elucidation of works of art. And perhaps I have underestimated Malraux's ambition in saying that works of art are to be used as historical evidence—the connection is more intimate. More than evidence in history, works of art are the selective embodiment of it, the chosen vessels of those few sacred moments when man stepped beyond himself in the act of creation. The aesthetic sense does not so much dramatize a vision of history as contain it. The images form a world in their own right. And the critic who has been closest to Malraux assures us that in the argument and composition of *Les Voix du*

Silence we are to take the notion of 'vision' quite literally, that the testimony is intended to be primarily visual. 'Le grand aveu des *Voix du Silence*, c'est que l'auteur eût souhaité manier des couleurs et des formes, non écrire des phrases...'[1] Whatever this may tell us of Malraux's actual intentions is uncertain. In any case it tells only a part of the truth. For often the conjunction of images seems created rather by the force of idea, or even by the intensity of language itself.

However, Picon's observation points like the 'cinematographic' quality of the novels to the extraordinary dependence of Malraux's mind on the succession of specific images, and one does feel that this flow of images has the power to take on a life, a continuity of its own. In the volumes that form a comprehensive collection of world sculpture the conceptual guidance is minimal and the flow of images is given its freedom without any startling consequence. Yet the natural ease and excitement in them is present, and it is as a maker of images more than of words that man defies his nothingness in *Les Noyers de l'Altenburg*. If one is to ask why the visual arts rather than any other have been selected, it is of course Malraux's instinctive excitement in the visual that is part of the answer. The rest may well lie in two qualities belonging pre-eminently to works of visual art. One is the simple fact of durability. The physical remnants of the past include the outlines of temples, thousands of miscellaneous artifacts, objects in clay and metal and stone that have survived when literature and music have not. Another lies in its universality and relative ease of approach. The educated and eclectic modern eye adjusts quickly to the most diverse and remote visual forms. The bizarre and monstrous are as easily assimilated as the recent and familiar. Nothing like the barrier of language or of the unintelligibility of musical conventions stands between us and some form of appreciation (however inadequate this may sometimes be). Finally, the observation of works of art is relatively quick and easy. To the habitual laziness of our nervous impatient sensibilities, *Njal's Saga*, or the *Vedas*, or the *Dream of the Red Chamber* are fairly arduous and time consuming—as is any serious involvement with oriental music.

[1] Gaëtan Picon, *Malraux par lui-même*, Paris, 1953, p. 123. 'The avowed purpose of *The Voices of Silence* is that the author has sought to arrange colours and forms, not to write phrases....'

Our halt in contemplation before a Khmer head, or a Carolingian ivory, may be long or a thing of the moment. The choice is our own, but the temptation to look quickly, and if informed passably well, to respond quickly, creates one of the standard problems of the museum-goer. The flutter of images before his eyes is too easily seen like the figures of a kaleidoscope, for a vivid but transitory moment. The succession of images sometimes seems more important to Malraux than the individual works themselves, and this rapidity of succession is made easier by the existence of the album of reproductions.

Because of the perfection of photographic techniques, the fine arts have 'found their printing press', and the consequences seem to Malraux analogous to those of that earlier invention. The knowledge of every form of the world's art has become available to all of us; our knowledge will no longer be narrow and parochial like that of the best nineteenth-century critics, even Baudelaire. No longer confined to our traditional corner in space and time we can regard the whole range of human accomplishment, and can trace the myriad patterns of the metamorphoses of forms. But more important than the spread of knowledge produced by the album is an alteration of the character of that knowledge. The anthology of images is a liberation from the physical constraint of an actual museum. In the museum there is an original detachment from context, and some aim at universality—the Louvre and all great museums seek a representative collection, and the Musée de l'Homme is there to remind us of the multiplicity of the forms of human genius. Perhaps the very range and variety of the museum underlines the expressive purity of objects seen in detachment. Time and space have obliterated context, and what is left to us is the staring face, the curious curve of a torso, the puzzling but eloquent design. Something in their isolation helps convey that sense of 'deeper life' that Malraux is seeking.

The album takes this process a step further: works are both more available than ever and doubly isolated from their origins, but are given a new context in their mere succession, in the complex interplay of image and idea within the anthologist's imaginary scheme. In a later section I shall discuss other effects of the isolation of works of art by the curator or anthologist. Here I only want to emphasize the obvious difference in the principle of selection and arrangement practised by the two. While the museum must rely upon its resources for selection, and arranges with a view to easy intelligibility, the maker of picture books may have infinite choice, and his selection and arrangement will be governed by an intellectual necessity or purpose. While the curator may only seek to make something look well, keeping in mind a rough chronology, or at most the orderly development of a school,[1] the book picture-makers' task is essentially eclectic, and almost inconceivable without intellectual or imaginative 'argument'. Even if the author hoped '... manier des couleurs et des formes, non écrire des phrases ...' such handling would still be in accordance with a conceptual scheme most naturally expressed in language.

Whatever the mixture of image and idea at the source of *Les Voix du Silence*, there is no doubt that its appeal is consistently both visual and literary. There is a direct demand made on visual perception; the reader is required to look and to see visual connections. But the force of the visual appeal is strengthened by a literary virtuosity which alternately suggests and proclaims what one must necessarily see. The fervour of the prose seems to invade the visual images themselves, with a consequent tension between the purpose of an example and the means by which it is conveyed. One effect of this dual method—the ideal effect —is insight linked to enthusiasm. Another may be a sense of uneasiness born of disproportion. In several ways the feeling grows that what the pictures tell and what the words do are not entirely the same thing. Two kinds of such disproportion are most obvious. For one thing the effects of actually looking lead in more directions than the argument itself—one sees the intended connection, but also many others. The concrete image suggests both the explicit comparison and quite different ones as well.

But more disturbing is the possibility that while some comparisons have an immediate and powerful impact, others do not get beyond the clichés of academic art history. In comparing the details of rocks by Leonardo with those of Filippo Lippi, or of a hand by Leonardo with one by Botticelli, Malraux simply makes the time-honoured distinction between linear and illusionist art; and he underlines an awareness which has already

1 Excepting, of course, many kinds of special exhibitions.

become habitual in suggesting the connection of older forms with an age of faith and those of Leonardo with a sheer delight in the display of skill. So when Malraux tells us ' " La Rencontre à la Porte d'Or" de Giotto n'est pas une supposition. Mais une Vierge de Lippi, de Botticelli, commencent à l'être; la "Vierge aux Rochers" l'est tout à fait. Un crucifix de Giotto est un témoignage; la "Cène" de Léonard est un conte sublime' (70).[1] We are not confronted with an unfamiliar idea, rather with a familiar idea in a rhetorically supercharged context; and from this context it may derive such power or concision, or startling sense of detail that the conventional has never seemed more significant or alive. We are here in the grip of a powerful imagination that can hold our attention and illuminate even the banal—through a gift that, whatever its matter, is essentially literary.

The ambivalent mixture and unstable balance of image and idea creates one of the serious obstacles to understanding *Les Voix du Silence* as an extended argument. To a large degree this difficulty lies in the rapidity of movement with which Malraux's mind darts from picture to historical generalization, from assertion to suggestion, re-examining and re-assembling his materials, embroidering them with analogies both familiar and remote. The quickness of movement and variety of matter, the elliptical style that suppresses prosaic connectives, can produce the effect of breathtaking, if possibly meretricious, dazzle. While such difficulties interfere with the orderly movement of ideas, the stylistic qualities themselves imply the secondary place that a development of a strictly logical kind has in Malraux's plan. The persuasion that he seeks is less a conviction of the mind than a response of the imagination, if possible the projection of the whole self into the state of mind he evokes. The reader's sensibility must be overwhelmed by the torrent of examples and allusions which substitute the procession of images and association of ideas for any more systematic manner of exposition.

In *Les Noyers de l'Altenburg* Malraux speaks of the special genius of the shaman—whose kind of magic survives in our

---

[1] 'The "Meeting at the Golden Gate" of Giotto is not a fiction. But a Virgin of Lippi or Botticelli commences to be; the "Virgin of the Rocks" is entirely. A crucifix of Giotto is a testament; Leonardo's "Last Supper" a sublime anecdote.'

world largely through the great artist. Without forcing an artificial comparison there is no doubt that Malraux regards his task in his aesthetic writings not only as closer to art than to academic historical study, but to a special kind of art which combines the urgency of the prophet's message with the rhetorical apparatus and eloquence of the great preachers. He intends not to demonstrate but to illumine, and seeks not the ordinary sort of intellectual conviction, but something akin to conversion. To illuminate, to transform, to excite, inflame—these are the aims of the sudden juxtapositions, the dazzling comparisons, the acrobatic play of words and images. Malraux presents himself in the double role of the seer, the visionary—and of the orator, in whose passionate verbal display a revolutionary spirit has lost none of its fervour. This is not to say that Malraux cannot use normal forms of evidence and logic when he chooses, or is ignorant of the actual historical background of the works he discusses. A quite individual treatment of the relation of works of art to their context has great importance when considering the contents of the Imaginary Museum.

It is within this enclosure of his own making that the visionary scheme unfolds—so uncertain in many of its implications. 'Malraux, se prépare-t-il à passer définitivement de l'action au spectacle, de la volonté à la représentation? En même temps que du tragique à la sérénité?[1] This question of Picon's is misleading in the suggestion that the world of the museum is without tragic implications of its own, or that the feverish style of Malraux's aesthetic writings conveys serenity. And as I have already said it seems a mistake to present this last metamorphosis of Malraux in such a sharply antithetical way. The old Malraux is contained, if altered, in the new. The metamorphoses of Apollo, the disintegrating image of Hermes on the coin—illustrated and documented on every level from the painfully familiar to the wholly fanciful—are themselves a fantastic journey of the imagination, a 'voie royale' of grander proportions, committed to many dimensions in space and time.

Only journeys no longer end in violence and death, or rather these are themselves absorbed into spectacle, into the whole pageant of humanity, in all its banality and barbarity, which

[1] 'Is Malraux preparing to pass definitively from action to visual spectacle, from will to representation? At the same time as from the tragic to the serene?'

Malraux has assembled in a place of quiet and safety, the museum, where the detached sensibility can play upon it. Yet in Malraux's case the sensibility is at fever heat, and the museum is a place of intoxication, of excitement in both the rich and strange, and in the hidden life of the ordinary. *Les Voix du Silence* proceeds from an intoxication with every form of human expression, from the desire to savour and compare every variety of expressive gesture. The museum is a connoisseur's fantasy—the world of an intensely romantic collector and critic. But the essential emotions of such a state belong to the private world of appreciation. Isolation is the core of the aesthetic attitude, and in this final incarnation it is Malraux rather than his heroes who is himself wholly isolated—he stands outside it all, the lone spectator in the splendid museum of his own creating—free to delight in, to compare, to celebrate. The atmosphere of hymn, of religious fervour rises about the lone observer awestruck before an immense and fantastic spectacle.

Picon suggests that for action *Les Voix du Silence* would substitute creation. This is of course the avowed intention. But the passion for comparison, the delight in detail, the acuteness of personal response—these are the qualities that dominate, and throughout the aesthetic works another kind of hero is suggested: not the creator but the perceiver, the critic, selector, compiler and guardian of the museum of humanity. The true aestheticism of Malraux's work declares itself not in its content, but in its point of view, in its unavoidable detachment, even in the elevation of the critic's or curator's task to the level of prophecy. It is in this that *Les Voix du Silence* is an aesthete's testimony.

II. In The Musée de l'Homme

'L E musée enseigne, hélas.' In its earliest incarnation in *La Tentation de l'Occident* the museum for Malraux is a lifeless storehouse, a funerary monument to the residue of the past. The sensitive oriental visitor to the Louvre is more concerned with what is seen through its windows. What the museum teaches, alas, is the heaviness and tedium of the past, and nowhere is the imaginative change in Malraux more significant than in the transformation of the museum into the scene of humanity's triumph. Certainly the notion of an ideal museum is the most important conceptual device of Malraux's aesthetic writings, and its central rôle in his scheme can be shown by setting down the argument of *Les Voix du Silence* in a series of propositions—admitting, of course, the violence that such an order does to Malraux's own method. The steps would be something like this: 1—The response to an anti-humanistic nihilism must come from the evidence about the true nature of man's character and works. 2—The most significant form of this evidence is in art, where the record is durable, and where the artist's insight grants the deepest knowledge of the character and creative powers of man. 3—However, this is not seen in all of art, but only in certain rare works which we call masterpieces, in which those creative powers have concentrated their most revealing moments, which can themselves be isolated, so the lineaments of this creative power can be identified and described. 4—The best way of doing so is through an 'imaginary

33

museum' in which these masterpieces are confronted with each other, and where we can grasp their essential message, stripped of the obscuring muddle of context. 5—From this confrontation and reading of the 'essential' comes a new realization, a vision of man conquering his destiny rather than the helpless victim of it. 6—So human history can be seen not as a fatality proceeding from a chain of causes, but as a flow of creative powers, both continuities and metamorphoses, absorbing and transcending circumstance.

In the pattern of this argument the rôle of the museum is not only crucial, but it is the only notion that has any direct bearing on the character of works of art as such. It creates a fundamental alteration of traditional aesthetic context by removing the work of art from its historical and personal situation. For this reason it has aroused the hostility of professional historians of art. To deprive a work of its natural context is to violate its character, to deprive it of its necessary explanatory background. Each work is part of a tradition, and in many respects unintelligible apart from it. Yet Malraux seems quite aware of this, even while making abstraction from context a primary function of the museum. This too has a validity as a critical procedure; it is quite natural to wish to isolate for special attention a work which stands beyond the common run in order to ask in what its uniqueness consists. And for this purpose one need not deny the importance of context, but merely set it aside. Malraux asks not what a work has in common with others of its kind, but what it possesses that is wholly its own.

Furthermore, the special conditions created by the Imaginary Museum seem exactly suited to the display of Malraux's own form of critical skill. 'Un souci d'arracher les choses à leur contexte naturel, de les transplanter, transposer, soutenues par uné volonté farouche qui ne s'embarrasse d'aucun remords, tel semble en définitive être le pli profond du génie de Malraux.'[1] It is this 'arrachement', with all its overtones of violence, with the 'volonté farouche' so ready to bend its materials to a pattern of its own, that provides Malraux with his 'comparaisons vertigineuses' and makes possible the relentless whirl of personal

[1] G. Duthuit, *Le Musée Imaginable*, Paris, 1956, Vol. II, 346–7. 'A concern to rend things from their natural context, to transplant and transpose them, sustained by an arrogant will which is not embarrassed by the least remorse, such seems definitively the profound bent of the genius of Malraux.'

insights and observations. The technique of *arrachement* also serves as the principle by which the Imaginary Museum is constructed. The notion of isolating the masterpieces of world art implies another, that the proper context of masterpieces is not the school of which they may form a part, or the social and personal background out of which they are created. The proper context of a masterpiece is others of its kind, and its proper kind is not the great company of lesser contemporaries, but other masterpieces. And this may be true however diverse their origins: 'Le dialogue des créations opposées est plus riche que la confusion du génie et ses épigones . . .' (607).[1] It is only in the presence of its true peers that the unique creative gesture is seen wholly and clearly, trimmed of the deadweight of background.

And emptied of subject matter. In the Imaginary Museum there are no more portraits, but only paintings. 'Il ne connut plus ni palladium, ni saint, ni christ, ni objet de vénération, de ressemblance, d'imagination, de décor, de possession: mais des images des choses, différentes des choses mêmes, et tirant de cette différence spécifique leur raison d'être' (12).[2] In Malraux's Museum these images which draw their strength from their nature as images somehow constitute a separate world of their own. As individual expressions they confront one another, displaying the individual triumphs of human genius; as a group they confront and arraign the inhuman order of things, a world created by sensibility and intelligence opposed to a world that is not.

The techniques of reproduction that have made the Imaginary Museum possible have had other effects, as far reaching with respect to works of art as that of universal distribution. For one thing, reproduction allows the free mixing of the most disparate genres. The album aligns the fresco with the canvas, enamels with tapestries, miniatures with public monuments. And this latter implies not only the mixing of genres, but an alteration of scale, where the levelling effect of the album's page may act either as the bed of Procrustes on which all works are tortured into an arbitrary size, or more imaginatively, as the means of

---

[1] 'The dialogue between works of quite opposed sorts is richer than the confusion of genius and its epigones.'
[2] 'It no longer knows palladium, nor saint, nor Christ, nor object of veneration, of resemblance, of imagination, of decoration or possession: but images of things, different from things themselves, and drawing from this specific difference the reason for their being.'

subordinating size to the more purely formal qualities of a work. Finally, and perhaps most significant of all, the camera's eye selects and isolates detail. All of the devices of the photographer's craft: focus and framing, light and shadow—are at the service of a selective process that may entirely alter the visual impression that we have of a work of art.

The usages and advantages of this are obvious and well known, especially with respect to sculpture: in the close inspection of the hidden detail, the dramatic articulation of a single line or plane, or what is possible with painting as well, the simple freeing of the significant detail from its background. The exploitation of this selectivity has not only made the range of comparison of the Imaginary Museum possible, but has left it open to a charge of free-wheeling eclecticism, and a sensationalism which seeks to startle by the discovery of resemblances in works which are basically dissimilar. Certainly many of the comparisons are chosen for their dramatic impact, as if the visual excitement had captured the imagination, and had diverted and complicated what might have been a fairly straightforward argument. But such cases are matched by others where the visual sense is carefully subordinated to the argument, and the examples are striking because of the perfect sensibility that informs them as illustration. The contrast of the rocks of Filippo Lippi with those of Leonardo (68–9), or the Gothic eye with the Romanesque (236–7) are not so much novel or striking in themselves as 'just right', the perfect visual example of an idea that was already formulated.

Of the many dangers in this kind of selectivity the temptation to the vividly put cliché is only one. The splitting up of the work of art into details, or the alteration of the camera's angle may result in comparisons so grotesque as to wholly distort the character of the work in question. The blown-up detail, the trick of lighting can falsify as well as illuminate. Malraux shows his awareness of this danger in his remarks on 'La Dame d'Elché': 'Le cadrage d'une sculpture, l'angle sous lequel elle est prise, *un étudié* surtout, donnent souvent un accent impérieux à ce qui n'était jusque-là que suggéré,' (19).[1] The temptation

[1] 'The framing (in a photographic sense) of a sculpture, the angle from which it is taken, a studiedness above all, often give an imperious accent to what was before merely suggested.'

36

is to find through such manipulations something which suggests false historical or psychological affinities, or to mistake the importance of a work through excess excitement in a particular detail. For all of his awareness of the dangers the temptations are clearly strong and one must ask of Malraux how misleading his abuse of the fragment, or the 'arty' photograph actually is. One could only answer properly by a detailed visual examination of the entire range of his examples. My own feeling is that the comparisons exist on every level of success and failure— from the really startling and illuminating to the banal, the doubtfully appropriate, even the perverse. But nevertheless when the chosen affinities are fanciful they are seldom genuinely deceptive; the detail is normally handled with a full sense that we are now to see something in a quite unusual way, just as the leaps through space and time involve no false suggestions of direct influence.

What Malraux has done is to have played upon the psychological affinities of works of art rather than the more conventional historical ones. 'Nous savons que l'art pathétique du maître de la Pietà de Villeneuve et l'art spécifique de Braque, si différent, ont les mêmes adversaires' (525).[1] This in a paragraph concerned with 'les arts d'assouvissement' works out a contrast by means of psychological categories, and creates the special affinity of two very unlike works (one Braque used is a bronze head of a horse) on the basis of such categories. And within the affinity claimed there is an inner contrast, between 'pathétique' and 'spécifique' which also exists on psychological grounds. The leap in time is to join two works through an act of opposition, however different the contexts, or the particular temptations they may have refused. They are united against the 'anti-art' of 'assouvissement' which panders to and flatters the tastes of an age. Yet they are only linked in a restricted sense. We can hardly doubt that on psychological as well as every normal historical ground the Villeneuve Pietà is directed to conditions quite different from those ('si différentes') of the very private art of Braque. (Not that in any normal sense the psychological and historical considerations can be mutually exclusive.) The chosen psychological connection touches only a fragment of the

---

[1] 'We know that the art of the pathetic of the Master of the "Villeneuve Pietà" and the art of the specific of Braque, so different, have the same adversaries.'

life of the paintings themselves. Such a remark may tell us something, however obliquely, about the psychological situation of the artist in two wholly different times, or about the external threat to the artist in any possible time, or even the essential negative gesture in both religious and modern art towards the claims of the world around them. But however interpreted it tells us nothing of any relevance to the specific character of these works of art.

The subordination of the historical connection to the psychological is surely one of the things Malraux means by a 'psychology of art'. In one sense, at least, psychology is opposed to history, in seeking below the level of the normal schema of historical circumstances that 'deeper life' which Malraux believes to show something universal and necessarily transcending the historical moment. In another sense, what psychology tells us is something about history itself; the timeless dialogue in the Imaginary Museum has its own bearing on the whole course of things. But the reading of this message is a subtle and elusive matter. It is worth emphasizing how easily, in the case of Braque and the Villeneuve Pietà, the essential connection between masterpieces can be of a minimal kind, even when the point in question is interesting enough and is the subject of extended discussion.

The slightness of impingement on particular cases is one reason for finding such connections suspect, or even frivolous. The extraordinary leaps in space and time, with a splendid indifference to actual dates and influences, the equal indifference to immediate context in order to rejoice in the remote comparison, the swift and uncritical shifting of artistic genres—all have left Malraux open to the charge of being 'anti-historical'. The imaginative bounds have seemed to his critics altogether too capricious; one is moved too suddenly from the obvious to the impossible, with the art of four cultures and three epochs handled in a subordinate clause. But with Malraux we can hardly regard this as sublime insouciance. The passing beyond traditional barriers and ignoring of traditional categories has the serious tone of a deliberate exercise in freedom. That this exercise is essential to his doctrine itself has been clearly caught by one of his critics: 'It (*La Psychologie de l'Art*) is in the first place unhistorical, or even anti-historical . . .

since Malraux finds that history imposes a tyranny on man, that it is something oppressive which he must escape, he attempts to free art from its bonds so far as possible.'[1]

What are the implications of this 'bondage of history' and the consequent need to escape from it? The proposition seems inherent in the character of the museum itself that the escape is to a timeless world where the 'eternal elements of art' coexist as a collective testimony regardless of the world of change and mortality without. Yet how can a 'psychology of art' have any real meaning if it denies the whole range of the human connections of a work in order to isolate it in a hermetic world? Does Malraux deny the importance of that enormous complex of human feelings out of which all art is inevitably shaped? If historical connections are subordinated to others does this mean they are considered irrelevant?

The answer to these latter two questions I think is clearly 'no'. For one thing he is intensely concerned, and often in great detail, with the particular qualities of historical periods, or with the personal background of the lives of artists—things we should normally consider part of the proper historical context of any work. In considering the development of great artists he insists on the importance of tradition and imitation. Giotto did not learn from the sheep, but from Cimabue (279). And clearly, in their wider sense psychological considerations do not exclude historical ones, for any intelligible picture of human psychology is inseparable from those habits, institutions, languages and traditions of which it is a part. Nor is this a separation which Malraux desires to make in any primitive way. The act of *arrachement* which creates the Museum does not so much destroy a connection, but create another. Malraux is deeply enough committed to expressionist presuppositions that the notion of the work of art as the key to the inner life of a culture is never far out of sight. This is of course as it should be in a work which purports to demonstrate something about the nature of the whole course of human history, using art, as I have said, as a form of evidence.

On the lowest level this co-existence of the Museum and the expressive function of a work could be a simple matter of critical pluralism. None of the connections of works that Malraux suggests need be exclusive of others; the relations of works of art may be of many kinds and described in a wide variety of ways. Malraux's critical impulse is to concentrate entirely on those features of objects of art, and the connections between them, that concern his own thesis, and without prejudice to other ways of seeing. The Museum is consequently not as hermetic as it seems. The dialogue within its walls is less a replacement than a complement to the multiple facets which works of art may already have—even if there is always persuasive force behind the claim that the features of works of art that the Museum displays are somehow more 'essential' and the connections between them more revealing than those more traditional, mechanical explanations, in which the work of art, like sugar and vitriol, is the product of its circumstances and not to be seen apart from them.

More than a mere critical pluralism, however, the claim of the Museum is to emphasize the fundamental duality of works of art.[1] Their life in the Museum is a different dimension from their life in time. In the latter they may be the expression of an epoch, the reflection of a culture, of individual skills and sufferings. In the Museum it is as if their essence were abstracted. Their value as Malraux's 'testimony' is in their generalized expression of human genius. And here the claims of historical context are not denied, but absorbed. Psychological and historical evidence are not at odds, but are involved in a common end. It is true that for Malraux psychological categories seem more natural, and psychological observations more urgent in their message. They are clearly to him not only the effective instruments of that deeper probe into works of art which is necessary for the Museum's testimony, but they also reflect the degree to which Malraux is obsessed with the psychology of artistic creation, and the artist as the hero of man's resistance to historical fatality.

Confusion can arise from this double reading of the art object. There is a psychological key which is the source of insight into the inner nature of a world, but the insight is not limited to the properties of the historical moment. The moment has disappeared into the man, and the man into his art; what

[1] This duality with respect to context is considered in more detail in section 4 of this chapter.

the art reveals is not only something of the sense of a particular place and time, but that it has a sense. The moment finds through style its place in the universal pageant; the particular is transcended without being lost. But Malraux is often quite careless as to whether it is the voice of the age which speaks through a work, or the private voice of the artist in its unique accent, or an intricate interaction of the two. The most intensive treatment is usually given to the personal and romantic features of an artist's work, seeing in Van Gogh and Rembrandt, Goya and Michelangelo, a superhuman image of the artist's power to recreate the world, to transform an external reality into his own. On the other hand we know nothing of the makers of Byzantine mosaics, or New Hebrides masks, or Khmer sculpture. The differences between them and those western artists whose character and development are well known to us are not the subject of a neat schematization. Where some artists are (or seem) quite at one with their world, and others engaged in conscious revolt, and where the conditions of artistic creation have been so various, there is bound to be a blurring of rôles, with a series of gradations between talk of artists in their own right and the world of which they are a part. Malraux responds to the variety of the rôles the artist has played in his culture with a gradation of accents, not with precise conceptual distinctions.

Perhaps it is part of Malraux's reaction to theories of historical fatalism that gives first place to the artist's heroism—a resurrection of the conventional Romantic elevation of the importance of genius. The *arrachement*, which provides the condition of entry into the Museum, is the isolation of the unique moment of creativity, that single expressive gesture which liberates the artist from the forms he has inherited and announces a form that is entirely his own—the creation of a style. The succession of such creative gestures, of the births of styles out of the demolition of their predecessors, forms in itself a special continuity, a 'history' so to speak, of creative acts, of moments of creative heroism, which runs parallel to history in the ordinary sense, again a complement rather than competitor.

So the artist, like his creation, both lives in time and steps beyond it, whether at one with his world or isolated by hostility and incomprehension. This dual existence is reflected in the simple dialectical pattern which is Malraux's model case for the creative act. The artist immerses himself in a tradition in order to move beyond it; he destroys in order to create a style of his own. Identification, destruction, recreation—these are the steps of the artist's dialectic. Although, of course, the great majority of artists never get beyond the first stage; they absorb a tradition in order to exploit and continue it. The creative gesture breaks through such conventions—as Goya broke through those of eighteenth-century decorative art. Malraux's most personal commitments seem behind the language which describes this situation with extraordinary vividness and power. On the dramatic crisis which precedes the destruction of a conventional style, on the violence of the demolition, on the tentative and delicate gropings that may foreshadow the new, Malraux rings multiple changes. From the most explosive break-through to the quite modest, a human event of the most significant and moving kind is lovingly and excitedly recorded, with a sensibility carefully attuned to every imaginable stage of an inner process. (I shall deal later with the problem of the hypothetical psychology this involves.) Malraux is emphatic about the variety of forms this may take. His heroes are Chardin and Vermeer, Latour and the Douanier Rousseau—as well as the great revolutionaries, Giotto and Masaccio, Goya and Manet. In every case and on every scale a private demolition takes place, and out of the imagination a new world comes to replace the old. But this is the study of artists, not of art, of the psychology of creativity rather than the character of the actual creation. A paradox may arise and contain its own elements of embarrassment, when these secret and turbulent moments, the private possessions of the psyche so dear to Malraux, can be reached only through the opaque objects hanging on the Museum wall.

2. STAGES AND METAMORPHOSES

This concentration on such an 'inner' quality of experience, and even the wild eclecticism with which the contents of the Museum are chosen still do not exclude from the Museum plan a loose but significant historical pattern. And in the three versions of the aesthetic works there is a clear movement towards a more rigid and orderly historical frame. What was perhaps implicit in *La Psychologie de l'Art*, more strongly suggested by

Les Voix du Silence, is now explicit and schematized in *La Méta-morphose des Dieux*.[1] The history of art as we know it forms a series of stages, of succeeding Weltanschauungen, and these are linked by an intelligible pattern of 'metamorphoses'. The process begins with what Malraux calls 'arts sacrés'—the arts of the ancient orient and middle east, above all, of Egypt. These are arts supremely devoted to the overwhelming majesty and total 'otherness' of the gods, arts of the eternal, hieratic and funereal.

Such arts with their utter remoteness from the human scale undergo the extraordinary metamorphosis from the world of the gods, to the humanization of divine forms. The smile of the Koré of Euthidikos breaks through the ritual pose, and the divine form is seen in the likeness of man. In classical art, which Malraux calls 'le Divin', forms are adapted to the human scale, the divine images endowed with human qualities, represented as sublime versions of ourselves. But in a succeeding metamorphosis this uneasy and marvellous equilibrium breaks down into the chaotic and unrationalized forms that accompany the collapse of the ancient world. The gods renew their sway in the 'Age of Faith', although they never break the spell of the humanized forms that they inherit. Nor is man's central position in the universe wholly displaced. Rather than the sense of a fatality without, which leaves man abject before supernatural forces, the Christian world places fatality within—man's fate may be both subject to the 'other' and dependent on himself.

This is a state which is secularized once again in a third metamorphosis, not discussed in the volume of *La Métamorphose des Dieux* that has been published, but whose character can be read in an earlier version in *Saturne*: 'Avec la Renaissance, l'Art était devenu distinct de ce qu'il exprimait. Il était passé du service de la foi à celui de la civilisation, d'une image parée que l'homme se faisait de lui-même' (S 146).[2] And from the Renaissance derives the extensive development of art as a source of pleasure, devoted largely to decoration, which, it is announced in *Les Voix du Silence* as in *Saturne*, is to crumble in the face of an

---

[1] I shall later sketch some of the developments represented in the changes from version to version.
[2] 'With the Renaissance art became distinct from that which it expressed. It had passed from the service of faith to that of civilization, to an ornate image that man had created of himself.'

43

ultimate metamorphosis which produces modern art—where Goya shatters the equanimity of the decorative tradition and Manet subordinates the content of the painting to painting itself. (*L'Exécution de Maximilien* de Manet, c'est le *Trois Mai* de Goya, moins ce que ce tableau signifie' (100)).[1] The final metamorphosis is to an art in which the only values are the formal values of pure painting. The kingdom of style has come into its own.

Although the whole evolution ends in a doctrine of the autonomy of art, in the metamorphoses that link the 'stages' of art's progress it is the historical imagination which seems to control the essential drama. The most vivid episodes in this progress are those that deal with the break-up of forms both in the gradual dying of the Greco-Roman world, and the collapse of neo-classical decorative values in the face of modern art. The cases are of course far from parallel: the former presents forms in the process of disintegration, yet inherited and used by others; the latter shows forms that are fossilized while something new is created beneath their surface. Malraux is fascinated by the destruction of forms, yet the whole notion of metamorphosis is meant to show that forms do not really disappear, but alter, that in their apparent disintegration new forms are taking shape which reflect either a quite different world-picture, or at least a quite different notion of why one should make images of the world. 'Les Métamorphoses d'Apollon' is a series of case-histories elaborating his theme of continuity through metamorphosis: the break-up of the image of Hermes on the stater of Philip II (of Macedon), the movement of the image of Apollo by way of Ghandhara into eastern art, and in the greatest detail the emergence of the Paleo-Christian out of the residue of the ancient world.

The Celtic and Germanic coin-makers are not seen as mere copyists who copied badly. 'D'une extrémité de l'Europe à l'autre, les barbares tenteront de recomposer l'Hèrmes selon leurs propres lois' (138).[2] The series of tortuous abstractions that replace the face, or the horse and charioteer, have a multiplicity of expressive gropings. But in all cases these distortions

---

[1] 'The "Execution of Maximilien" of Manet is the "Third of May" of Goya, less what the latter means.'
[2] 'From one extremity of Europe to another, the barbarians attempted to recompose the Hermes according to their own laws.'

show the moment of creation, rather than a simple clumsiness in imitation. Whether or not we can accord them any particular artistic merit, or find for them any place in a growing school or tradition now lost in the chaos of barbarous times—even if they are forms without a future, without consequences—their validity as testimony to a profound continuity is unimpaired. And their real value lies in the fact that through whatever alterations of form they maintain their power to express: 'Du moins ses figures montrent-elles la conquête de l'Hermès macédonien par la volonté barbare avec assez de netteté pour éclairer dans la décomposition des formes antiques depuis Elche jusqu'à Loung-Men, la part de leur métamorphose et celle de leur agonie' (142).[1]

The oriental adventures of the Apollo figure are of course a quite different matter in having artistic consequences of great (if often disputed) importance. For this study Malraux has an *embarras de richesse*, and he has created of it a splendid visual procession, with a profusion of connotative echoes, of startling suggestions and confrontations, as when the smiling angel of Rheims faces its Ghandharan semblance (158–9). There is also no doubt that some genuine chain of historical connections lies behind the continuity described, and at moments Malraux's visual and historical imagination seem brilliantly fused, with the splendid succession of images (146–71) and the dexterous moves through space and time illuminating rather than confusing. The power and range of imagination are seductive, and redolent of the excitement in adventure of those earlier exotic journeys—*La Tentation de l'Occident* and *La Voie Royale*. Yet splendid and moving as they are, both in bit and in total spectacle, these historical episodes read more like romances than like evidence. Their very personal intensity clouds our sense of their precise relevance. Even accepting the case of Apollo as a proper demonstration of the metamorphosis principle, the connections described may be no more than a happy accident of cultural history, a dramatic and fruitful conjunction that feeds the imagination, but hardly gives us the adequate ground of general conclusions.

[1] 'At the least these figures demonstrate the conquest of the Macedonian Hermes by the barbarian will with sufficient precision to make clear, in the breaking down of ancient forms from Elche to Loung-men, both the extent of their metamorphosis and that of their agony.'

A far more complicated case is that of the decline of the ancient world. It has always had a central place in the historical imagination, has been the critical episode for those speculative systems that would explain the cycles and patterns of history, and of course it has left an enormous and well-examined residue in works of art. Considering Malraux's avowed intention of 'refuting' Spengler, the purpose of this particular study is to show conclusively that there is no real evidence of the death and disappearance of forms that would justify fatalistic Spenglerian theses about the course of history. Rather there is a continuous process of reinterpreting and transforming. Such a view commits Malraux to a critical upgrading of the successor styles to the classical world: Byzantine and Paleo-Christian, barbarian and Gallo-Roman art. Of course the wheel of fashion has long since turned from the time when these were considered wholly retrograde and insignificant forms, but Malraux wishes to go further and establish them as worthy successors. In doing so he sees in art a psychological history. In the catacombs, at Palmyra, in the Fayum, in Gallo-Roman art, Malraux sees the infiltration of the other-worldly and oriental, quietly asserted through the forms of Roman art, but speaking with another accent. 'Sur l'empire mourant les dieux rétablissaient leur invincible domination. Ce qui mourait avec lui, c'etait l'art profane. Les faces souriantes de l'Attique et d'Alexandrie, les faces assurées du Capitole n'étaient pas moins étrangères au désert, à la forêt, aux catacombes, au monde nocturne des astres et du sang, que Plutarque à Saint Augustin' (184).[1]

Characteristically, the detailing of this particular metamorphosis is not primarily the record of a continuing tradition, or the tracing of similarities or continuities of styles; it is rather an essay of exceptional intensity on the nature of the psychological crisis of a culture, and the possibilities of artistic response to that crisis. It is the outbreak of a new gesture in response to an altered spiritual condition, or the detection of the altered attitude behind the facade of traditional forms that involves both Malraux's imagination and his critical eye. The far-flung nature of the

[1] 'Over the dying empire the gods re-established their invincible rule. That which was dying with it was profane art. The smiling faces of Attica and Alexandria, the stern faces of the Capitol were as much strangers to the desert, to the forest, to the catacombs, to the nocturnal world of blood and stars, as Plutarch to St. Augustine.'

material may make some of the comparisons less than subtle, and the actual historical conclusions may be more conventional than the manner that evokes them, but Malraux's dramatic sense catches with penetrating sympathy and great vividness the cross-purposes involved in the historical moment stretched taut by the conflicting claims of the world and its Maker, as artistic forms slip by awkward and tentative degrees into some expression of the supernatural. Malraux gropes for those alterations of feeling and style that change senators into apostles, and that produce the evolution of the Agrippa 'assuré' into the Baptist of Rheims (216–17). The creative act that has a single inheritance may yet tremble between the claims of disparate world orders. For Malraux this is a study that moves from the expression to the inner life. Here also, the camera's eye is the servant of insight. The fragments of those transitional centuries lend themselves to its isolating power, and the play with shadows suggests the very Weltanschauung of the works themselves (cf. 235). The metamorphosis that receives most excited treatment in the search for psychological reasons also produces the most overtly expressionist handling of detail.

Both this expressionist concentration in the startling or exotic, and the critical upgrading of barbarian and other transitional works challenge certain habitual normative concepts of what is the true nature of a masterpiece, or the proper criterion of artistic excellence. For centuries our taste has been formed by the models of Greco-Roman and Renaissance art; we have regarded their harmonious rendering of the human form as an unmatched achievement, and any falling away from such standards, as in the decline of Roman art, as the result of simple incompetence. This is the theme of Berenson's essay on the decline of form, *The Arch of Constantine*, where he traces the effects of the use of plaster overlays, with the consequent loss of those modelling techniques which are fundamental to the artist's skill. Berenson presents this technical decline as the concomitant of social change, when the influence of the metropolis is no longer maintained throughout the empire:

> The substratum of art, the shapes, techniques and iconography thus remained uniform in Christian countries down to and through the Merovingian period. The differences, ever on the increase as from Constantinople we travel westward and northward, were

47

not due to the intrusion of new methods and new ideals. They resulted from the varying degrees of incompetence where the magnetic energy of the Eastern Empire failed of its effects and native artisans of remote regions, left without metropolitan guidance, were reduced to their primitive, pre-Hellenistic craft habits.[1]

Of course a judgment of this sort presupposes not only the existence of certain artistic canons which concern the skill implicit in representational powers, but an historical assumption, that only in the highest civilizations is there any possibility that man's creative powers can reach the supreme heights and produce masterpieces which are worthy of our whole admiration. Other works may appeal to the vagaries of jaded tastes, to a curiosity arising from boredom, and it is consequently a vice of the present age that we respond so easily to the primitive and barbaric, the surrealist and degenerate. The eclecticism of the present moment is that of a confused and chaotic world which has somehow lost that traditional sense of standards that has informed the best of human sensibility. Our sympathy is too ready to find moving the grotesque and marginal. And the confusion of the spirit has produced a confusion of the eye:

> What has recently happened is that the artist and public have had their visual convictions confused and destroyed by being suddenly presented with originals and reproductions of every kind of representational artifact, brought by explorers, by archaeologists, by dealers, and written up by the critics of the day as being as good as, if not better than the masterpieces we Western peoples had been admiring for centuries, nay, for thousands of years. These amusingly infantile products. . . .[2]

Implicit here is a rejection not only of an interpretation of late Roman art and its successor styles, but an attack on the principle of the Imaginary Museum. Berenson denies the artistic value of the 'expressive', as well as the possibility of comparing the products of dissimilar cultures. Yet he is profoundly aware of the multiplicity of forms operative within a single culture at a single moment, and the decline of the empire is rich in examples of this stylistic co-existence. One comparison that Berenson offers is of two portrait heads of Licinius, one a skilful, realistic but quite conventional Roman portrait, the other

[1] Berenson, *The Arch of Constantine*, New York, 1943, p. 8.
[2] pp. 62–3.

crudely worked in porphyry, forceful and barbaric. To Berenson the former represents the successful maintenance of the standards and skills of a cosmopolitan civilization, the other a relapse into inadequate technique and debased conception. But the latter is unquestionably the more striking, the more exciting and memorable. Above all, it is the more expressive, and would surely appeal to Malraux, as to most modern observers, as a more revealing and compelling work than the pedestrian Roman portrait. Just as the art of the Fayum may appeal more profoundly than the technically polished art of Pompeiian frescos.

The interesting feature of Berenson's argument is that he appears to base his preference primarily on technical considerations, on the fact of the presence of certain plastic skills. But the ultimate ground of it is the assumption of the precise correspondence between such skills and the living fact of a superior civilization. The technical argument is only the indirect means of presenting an historical argument, of a kind quite similar to Malraux's, asserting or implying a total historical judgment in the aesthetic perception. Only the opposite conclusion is reached: Berenson's judgment is normative and restrictive, based on the belief in one essential artistic and cultural inheritance; Malraux is universal and eclectic, responsive to whatever style or tradition reveals any significant feature of man. A dispute of this sort could not, of course, be settled by the appeal to evidence and perhaps not by the use of argument of any kind. The opposition of two images of man, and the consequent exaltation of those creative works that accord with those two images, is the kind of difference from which there is little appeal. The presuppositions of each exclude the other. The judgment implied in one image of man involves a commitment, and the conflict of two such visions requires an appeal to the imagination rather than to logic or fact. And apart from the persuasive power which may affect one's response to such an appeal, the literary powers involved in constructing and evoking such an image of man, and apart as well from the sense of reality invoked in giving such an image a foundation in one's analysis of the human condition, one is left with the fact of the visionary, where the vision itself, whatever its regard for the orthodox methods of historians, is conceived in historical terms. A concept of art rests upon one of history, and that in turn on one of man.

The opposition of Malraux and Berenson even in two forms of aesthetic humanism is like that traditional conflict of Romanticism and Classicism, a total opposition of choice, feeling and imagination.

3. THE AUTONOMY OF ART

Another important element in the remarks of Berenson lies in his distaste for modern art. To his committed sensibility, its distortions of form and disregard of traditional technique are base and foolish—an offence to his whole world view. For Malraux, however, it is not only the last (so far as we can possibly know) but perhaps the most important stage to which the metamorphoses have brought us. The succession of metamorphoses is represented as a genuine progression, the gradual liberation of the artistic powers of man from subservience to other ideals —from religion and philosophic doctrine, and the demands of realism, decoration or sentiment. The triumph of modern art is the revelation of its autonomy: 'Il existe une valeur fondamentale de l'art moderne... c'est la très vieille volonté de création d'un monde autonome, *pour la première fois réduite à elle seule*' (614).[1] With the coming of the museum which removes the painting from any but an artistic context, and the simultaneous breakdown of the traditional representational ways of seeing an object in the art of the late nineteenth century, painting has entered into its proper autonomy—an autonomy perhaps implicit if never asserted in previous ages. The isolation of the museum has made it possible to see art as art. And the gradual self-assertion of the artist—a self-assertion both visual and personal—has aided the process. For only so isolated and assured of its independence can the grandeur of the artist's challenge to reality be expressed and finally understood. '... à travers les quelques objets qu'il produit ou reproduit, c'est une reprise totale du monde que vise l'acte créateur.[2] To Malraux this renewal must be a double one, both that implicit in the single work, and the more complete version of the same in the collective world of the museum wall.

[1] 'There exists one fundamental value in modern art; it is the very ancient will to create an autonomous world, *now, for the first time contained strictly within itself.*'
[2] Sartre, 'Qu'est-ce que la littérature', *Situations*, II, Paris, 1948, p. 106. 'Through whatever objects it produces or reproduces, the creative act aims at a total renewal of the world.'

The notion of an 'autonomous world' of art, in which works are seen and judged entirely in their own terms, by formal criteria which belong to their own world, and where the painter's aim is to impress only an audience of his peers, both fits a modern prejudice and accords with modern practice. Whatever the role of aesthetic theory in our appreciations, we habitually accept a bland liberalism that admits an infinity of aesthetic standards. And we have rationalized our natural passivity before the isolated object so far as to give it its own way and allow it to formulate its own rules. For Malraux this situation is an ambiguous triumph. In theory it gives to all the varieties of human genius their pride in independence. Human genius, through acts of pure expression, may have created something of its own from the chaos that surrounds it, a salvation by means of the power of attaining aesthetic form.

But it is an aestheticism both extravagant and impossible to maintain. If one held such a pure and uncompromising doctrine of the autonomy of art, with such an exalted view of its place in human affairs, it would represent an eroding away of any other human values—a cutting off of any other possible purposes to human existence beyond self-expression for its own sake. An expressionist theory of human nature would follow an expressionist aesthetic. Yet it is clear that Malraux has no such rigorous intentions, and would not wish to accept such constricting consequences. There is not only the intimate and lively sense with which Malraux grasps the range of human thought and feeling connected with a work of art, but there is also throughout his work a persistent metaphysical hunger, a nostalgia for the 'absolute'. And this gives the greatest eloquence to his own historical imagination when it reaches those worlds most remote from our own indulgent liberalism—when it is confronted by the giant images of the Buddha, or with Byzantium, or the ruler of Lagash. In the face of these an accommodation to a doctrine of the 'autonomous realm' would seem awkward to say the least. The creative act seems in some way to reach out beyond itself, to catch some quality of the eternal order of things, and in a manner that is not merely the making of self-contained images of the visual world. To this reach Malraux's own sympathies, however inconsistently and uneasily, respond.

Another problem in the doctrine of the autonomy of art is

that posed by M. Merleau-Ponty.[1] To him Malraux's Museum is not only anti-historical but anti-naturalist as well. More significant than the evasion of conventional historical method is the divorce of the artist from his natural context in the human community, and the divorce of the work he does from its natural context in the visual world. Malraux has deprived the artist's perception of its matter-of-fact place in the world of things, replacing by visionary extravagance in a mystical presentation of the artist's insight the visual reality of what artists really do. By creating his detached and artificial world of images isolated by museum walls, he has created a monstrosity.

According to Merleau-Ponty the notion of a special autonomous realm of art must be corrected by a more empirical account of the creative process, showing the artist and his perceptions in a natural context, where all language and all symbols are part of the living continuum of things and events. As all language derives its meaning from its verbal and human context, so also are all expressive acts inseparable from their matrix in a particular tradition, human environment, and in the elaborate conditioning of the visual sense. Through the technique of 'arrachement' and the special character of the Museum Malraux has created an artificial separation of the work from living humanity, and in doing so has given a specialized view of art history in which objects of art have 'connections' of a special and mysterious kind—all a distortion of what works of art really are and do.

I have already showed how some difficulties arise from the application of this argument to historical context—the Museum is not always as hermetic as it seems. But the force of Merleau-Ponty's argument is almost entirely in a detailed study of normal perception, and a demonstration that the artist's way of seeing is only a refined and specialized version of the ordinary. This account is interesting and persuasive, and it is easy enough to agree with him in his contention that what an artist's eye and hand may do are simply extensions of our normal faculties and skills. But what his argument cannot do is show how such empirical accounts of perception, or of the working of hand and eye in the physical world, in any way explains how it is that the

[1] M. Merleau-Ponty, 'Le langage indirect et les voix du Silence', Les Temps Modernes, June, July, 1952.

creation of works of art really does differ from all of the other activities to which it is analogous. Nor can it help us understand how of several occasions of such activity, the results may vary from daubs through the pastiche of competent Sunday painters, to minor school works, and in the end to great masterpieces. From the point of view of the extension of our normal faculties and talents these occasions must be much the same. Of course one can claim that the great masterpiece is produced by the most sensitive and discriminating eye, the most skilful and disciplined hand. But this argument clearly involves circularity or special pleading. The same education of eye and much the same skills may have gone into two works of a painter, yet only one of them be a masterpiece, or of two painters of the same school, one worthy, the other a master. Something else differentiates the latter, and it is not something which empirical analysis reveals.

Perhaps this is so because there is no way in which observation can be brought to bear on the precise features of the creative process itself, or a proper method of empirical description devised to account for the stages of such a process. All attempts to account for the difference between the artist and the ordinary man, or the great artist and the average, involve an argument that moves back from the finished work, that is by its nature necessarily hypothetical, an imaginative projection which can only begin with the one relevant 'fact' in the case, the object of art itself. As an imaginative projection such an account will always be metaphorical and oblique, will never try to grasp the impossibly remote process by which the masterpiece emerged, step by step, out of the infinitely complex interplay of hand and eye, in the now vanished conditions of time, place, and individual circumstance. We will always know too little of these things to make explanation satisfying, and even if we knew vastly more, the essential differentiating qualities that distinguish between the great and the ordinary might well elude us. They might even be wholly indistinguishable by whatever empirical criteria we devise. What is left to the critic fascinated by the creative power of genius is his own power of imagination— penetrating as best it can the body of works that genius has left behind, explaining whatever resemblances and connections seem relevant.

Consequently Malraux might well agree with some of the

53

observations on which Merleau-Ponty's criticism is based, without drawing from it the same series of conclusions—through making clear that his main purpose has not been an empirical description of the creative process (although where he has touched on this, as in the case of Goya, he has not ignored personal history or visual environment). Nor is there any reason why he should, to establish his own image of the artist's conquest, be concerned with the ways in which the object of art is enmeshed in the ordinary world of things and events—matters more relevant to the biographer and social historian or the student of the psychology of perception. Rather it is the capacity of works of art to escape and transcend that circumstantial world which makes them something so wholly extraordinary as to be considered on their own terms. The studies of remote forms of art show this transcendent power may be undiminished when the circumstances of their creation remain unknown; and the universality of human genius declares the presence of the creative act under almost all imaginable circumstances. Furthermore, the effect of time is to obliterate context, leaving the work to speak for itself. The Museum is, in a way, a quite natural creation, formed by our own awareness of the selective process which shapes the residue of time, just as any doctrine of 'the autonomy of art' is created by the awareness that great art is a special kind of thing, not entirely explainable in terms of other phenomena.

In Malraux's attempt to relate the separate world of art to the obvious fact of its context, and to its use as historical evidence, there are many obscurities and unresolved paradoxes. Above all the consequences of the kind of autonomy asserted by the modern artist seem unexplored. (Although perhaps the second volume of *La Métamorphose des Dieux* will specify some of them.) Certainly his own version of the doctrine of the autonomy of art is neither clearly stated nor consistently applied. Although this might be an improper requirement for a doctrine of this kind, and it might be possible to suggest that any doctrine which asserts the 'autonomy of art' has no intention of doing so literally. It is a figurative, or at least, a relative autonomy that may be claimed, and even this only to such extent that traditional or habitual connections of works of art with their world are subordinated to the essential 'apartness' of masterpieces.

4. EXPRESSIONISM, HISTORICISM AND THE SENSE OF CONTEXT

One final, and perhaps most serious attack on the composition and character of the Imaginary Museum is based on its expressionist and historical presuppositions. Professor Gombrich, in his recent devastations of Malraux, has argued that the expressionist assumptions inevitably commit themselves to a fatalistic historicism in which all works are confined to their own frame of reference. So in spite of avowed intentions Spengler's critic is in the end Spengler's victim, unintentionally committed to a blind fatalism. Gombrich[1] relates these expressionist presuppositions to the discovery of exotic and primitive arts in the early years of the century, which allowed the imagination to multiply the ways in which forms could mirror the 'soul' of a culture, an intoxication with new arts leading to '. . . daily discoveries of new worlds, the hourly transvaluation of all values.' (Hans Tietze—and the latter phrase is of course an echo of Nietzsche.) The proper corollary of these discoveries of new worlds was an acceptance of the fact that they must be understood in terms that are wholly their own and are not translatable into the values of artistic traditions that are alien to them. Thus African sculpture must be seen in terms of the values belonging to its own world, not measured by the norms of classical or Renaissance forms, and the only means of comparing their existence as masterpieces is by asking how well they express or epitomize the unique qualities of their own world.

Consequently, expressionism, the doctrine that works of art are significant insofar as they express human feeling and reveal the particular qualities of an age, and historicism, the seeing of all experience and all manifestations of a culture in historical, hence time-bound and relativist terms—are inevitably linked.[2]

[1] E. H. Gombrich, 'Malraux and the Crisis of Expressionism', *Burlington Magazine*, December, 1954. See also *The Observer*, 9 October, 1960.

[2] Here I am of course referring to the wider and traditional meaning of 'historism' (the 'Historismus' of Meinecke, etc.), not the special meaning attached by K. R. Popper: any theory which claims to discern general laws in history. 'Historicism', used by Auerbach in the passage in the next paragraph avoids this ambiguity, but has not entered into general usage. There is perhaps some uneasiness in Prof. Gombrich's own handling of the term, for insofar as he is concerned with the problem of historical knowledge, with the dilemma of the historicist immured within his own frame of reference, it must be the former, traditional meaning which he has in mind. Yet in attacking the more visionary elements in Malraux he shares the tone of Popper's attack on the anti-rationalist character of his own sort of 'historicist' enemy.

The connection implies a fatal barrier to any true knowledge of the art of the past, and an attempt on such premises to understand arts other than our own involves a contradiction. So Malraux, in his attempt to utilize expressionism while evading the consequences of historicism in his timeless Museum, represents a 'crisis of expressionism'. And the museum itself, filled with a rich variety of expressive moments is a 'temple dedicated to a myth'. For if all forms of expression mirror their own age, then the Museum for all its universal claims will mirror its own age, its universality merely relative to our own time-bound point of view. The historian immured in his own can never really grasp the 'otherness' of other cultures—the notion of expression as the essence of art requires in the end a denial of the possibility of communicating what art expresses—and the art historian is caught up in his own version of Epimenides' paradox (a Cretan stating that 'all Cretans are liars'), falsifying his every assertion through the point of view from which it is made.

'General and aesthetic historism,' says Auerbach, 'is a precious (and also very dangerous) acquisition of the human mind. . . .'[1] And one danger of aesthetic historicism is possibly such a cultural isolation as Gombrich discovers hand in hand with expressionist fancy. For Gombrich, doctrine, imagination and cultural atavism are in Malraux the enemies of a proper empirical method in history. Malraux is committed by tastes and presuppositions to a cultural relativism complemented by the expressionist excitement in a remote range of images that deeply or obscurely stir the fancy. But the fact of such a danger cannot inhibit the realization that both of these doctrines have a powerful claim upon us, however we are to square them with each other. Furthermore, the strange and remote will appeal to us through a mixture of similarity and difference: 'De l'histoire des civilisations mortes, comme de l'ethnographie des peuples mourants, nous attendons qu'elles nous enseignent ce qu'est l'homme lorsqu'il ne nous ressemble pas' (M 32).

While the comparison with Epimenides may be fanciful, or might suggest unnecessary dimensions to the problem, the historicist dilemma Gombrich describes is one of the standard difficulties of any theory of historical knowledge, and in no way

[1] Eric Auerbach, 'Vico & Aesthetic Historism' in *Scenes from the Drama of European Literature*, New York, 1959, p. 184.

restricted to art history. However, the doctrine of expressionism, with its reliance upon the direct and imaginative character of aesthetic experience makes the problem more immediate, more directly involved with human feeling than events of the past that exist only as records or remote memories. The work of art has a more ambiguous life, existing as it does both in the past and in the present, the subject of both immediate apprehension and historical speculation. Whatever the attendant dangers, one of the durable legacies of historicism would seem to be that we have acquired an aesthetic double vision: we have learned to see all works of art as part of their historical epoch, and all historical epochs as independent in their standards—yet all of these as co-existent and somehow equal in the mind's eye. (A co-existence which, incidentally, does not deter one from distinguishing between greater and lesser traditions.) This is a double focus that Malraux clearly exploits. On the surface his *arrachement* seems anti-historicist in the apparent denial that works of art must be seen in terms of their cultural context, with the isolation of the museum a denial of history or a struggle against it. In reality, Malraux has carried the principle of aesthetic historicism one step further; the individual masterpiece is the summation of the values implicit in a whole civilization, and the parade of masterpieces in the Museum is a succession of spiritual essences testifying to man's accomplishment in the sum of historical moments. Man is immersed in history, yet steps beyond it. But always, the step beyond implies many things about what has gone before; in stepping out of their world, works of art somehow carry much of it with them.

Yet Gombrich has touched on a disturbing reality. There is an ambiguity in Malraux that can amount to anguish, and which dramatizes this double-focus of historicism itself. One is forced by the spectacle of history to accept the variety of values mankind has asserted for itself, and yet one is tempted by certain patterns in that spectacle to find other values over-arching and inclusive, more universal than the values of a particular time. And properly codified these may become the values of a particular time, limited as any other feature of that time to its own historical moment.

Gombrich has observed that often the long lists of names in

Malraux seem merely decorative, except insofar as they are incantations recited to reassure the writer of their reality, and hence re-inforce the tenuous hold of the historicist-expressionist on the reality of other cultures. But this is to misunderstand the purpose of the incantations (I shall discuss them in the final chapter) and to mistake a personal isolation for an historical one. The assumption is too easily made that Malraux fears this failure of communication which leaves us culturally immured. Malraux is at least quite willing to accept the otherness and remoteness both of cultures and of objects. On the other hand, the fact of ultimate personal isolation is an inevitable fact of the human situation—Malraux's works from the beginning insist on this. We may occasionally and for a moment break through this isolation with sudden dramatic moments of personal contact (various episodes in the novels) or through those leaps of the imagination that respond to those great works in which we recognize our humanity.

To the tangle over historicism Gombrich proposes a common-sense solution, which rejects the 'adolescent "all or nothing" attitude which colours so much of the writing of Malraux's generation'. This 'adolescent attitude' can of course be nothing but any possible critical attitude that implies personal 'engagement', and Gombrich is making a plea for the detachment of pure scholarship. With works of art we 'improve our understanding by trying to restore the context', a task properly performed in libraries, not in the fancies of dilettantes. In some cases this may be relatively easy, but in others, those of civilizations remote from us, it is possible only with a great deal of labour—it is only too obvious that some cultures of the past are more accessible to the understanding than others. This argument may hang uneasily on what is meant by 'understanding', and Gombrich quotes Malraux approvingly as calling our age one ready to 'admire all it does not understand'—as if he too were unconsciously in need of the explanatory context his own construction denies him. Yet this hardly exhausts the possibilities of 'understanding' a work of art, and two issues remain pressing and unsettled, both bearing on the difference between Gombrich's and Malraux's notions of 'understanding': 1— Does Gombrich himself misunderstand, or ignore, the real purposes of Malraux's 'arrachement', and 2—does his commonsense solution, useful as it may be for the kind of knowledge we often seek, actually solve or evade the art-historian's version of Epimenides' paradox?

In the former case, Gombrich clearly ignores the seriousness of Malraux's purpose in detachment from context simply because the results are disorderly, and conducive to romantic excess. But to ignore in such a way leads to two kinds of misunderstanding. One of these I have already pointed out in showing that Malraux means no denial of the sense of context but only to look beyond it, or to hold it in abeyance for specified purposes. The other is to imply a contempt for any insight into a work of art that does not stem from a proper historical perspective. And this is not only to distort Malraux, but to narrow seriously the possible ways of experiencing and talking about works of art. No reaction or comment would be relevant except that of professors, or professional connoisseurs. The fresh reaction, or direct visual response would reflect the ignorance of children or hopeless amateurs. The consequence is an impoverishing reductivism in which the relation of professional standards to the experience of objects of art is grotesquely distorted. The refutation of expressionism might, if carried out thoroughly, imply the divorce of the art object from any other human context than the operation of the visual mechanism with its attendant psychological oddities, and the study of historical and iconographic evidence. And there is the further danger of assuming that adequate professional knowledge will really be able to tell us exactly what works of art are like. To insist too much on the absolute authority of historical knowledge would be to seek neatly to outline a shadow, and to replace the curious, awkward, many-sided thing, which arouses us in such a variety of ways, with a conceptually adjustable academic abstraction. And as for the paradox of historical knowledge, we may well admit the utility of commonsense solutions in practice, without for a moment supposing that they simplify the complex interplay of perception, personal response, and information that compose any 'understanding' of a work of art.

In all moves that propose commonsense solutions to intellectual paradox, like Moore's defence of the reality of the external world, or even Dr Johnson on Berkeley, there is a healthy exasperation, with contempt for the excesses of either logic or imagination. And the same commonsense approach regards with natural suspicion an attempt to find in art any overall meaning or message. That Malraux should seek such a meaning seems bizarre and foolish, a spiritual hubris which leads directly to nonsense. But this is not an accusation which has been clearly or consistently maintained. Malraux's Museum may be a temple dedicated to a private work of the imagination, but hardly to a myth in any conventional expressionist-historicist manner. It seems, in fact, to share Gombrich's wish to evade the puzzle of historicism, but by conceptual device rather than the hack at the Gordian knot. For Malraux, historicism and expressionism are legacies, not doctrines—never rationalized or explicitly defended they are simply a part of the inherited substratum of his thought. But insofar as the conceptual device of the Museum is relevant to them, it wishes to go beyond the commitment to historical relativism, or the unintelligibility of the purely expressive. And it does so by inventing a special context which may incorporate or ignore at will the original one—and entirely for the sake of what seems the essential message of the work itself. So the dual face of the Museum with respect to history, both incorporating it and stepping outside it by detaching its greatest works from time, may offer difficulties of a 'have your cake and eat it too' variety. If not as the vehicle of the 'expressionist crisis'.

In fact, what Malraux seems to have done, is to preserve far better than the scholarly detachment of Gombrich would do, the double existence of works of art. For the ideal scholar's detachment involves him in some degree of denial of his own self, or any personal consciousness of his own rôle or moment in history. Standards in scholarship require the repression of any subjective element, the effacement of the self before the uncontaminated material, made safely a part of the past and beyond the reach of dangerous fancy. To regard history without involvement in it, to be wholly observer and never actor, may be a useful artifice and a worthy discipline for historical studies, but must necessarily ignore the historian's presence as a human being, his own involvement in the history he must record. But this is an intricate problem, 'And the question still is as it was then,' as Nietzsche said of *The Birth of Tragedy*, 'how to view scholarship from the vantage of the artist and art from the vantage of life.'

In complete opposition to this depersonalization of the historian and critic Malraux presents a 'critique engagée', based on the acceptance of oneself as an historical entity, committed to an understanding of works and events among which the observing self has an inescapable part. The experience of history and of art cannot be impersonal (they would be so at the expense of being inconsequential), and the 'adolescent "all or nothing" attitude of Malraux and his generation' partakes of an involvement in history that Sartre has described as the essential experience of that precise generation:

> L'historicité reflua sur nous; dans tout ce que nous touchions, dans l'air que nous respirions, dans la page que nous lisions, dans celle que nous écrivions, dans l'amour même, nous découvrions comme un goût d'histoire, c'est-à-dire un mélange amer et ambigu d'absolu et de transitoire.[1]

This describes the experience behind *Les Voix du Silence* as well as providing a key to the critical principles with which it operates, both the intensity of historical sense behind the examination of art and the fact that we 'are situated' in a profound and inevitable sense when we reflect on the historical moment or confront an object of art.

Yet some corner of doubt may remain as to whether the Museum in evading the dilemma of historicism may not also destroy that immediacy of experience and perception which a 'critique engagée' requires. In what way, and with what consequences, can one really say in Malraux's Museum that 'we are situated'? I shall try to show later that this is a personal and perhaps tragic dilemma for Malraux, and that the Museum, poised uneasily between the 'absolute' and the 'transitory', must strive to satisfy the needs of both, and under such pressures as are perhaps destructive of its original purpose. However, at no point does Malraux really wish to abandon a critical attitude which depends on the fact of art's existence in some direct conjunction with ourselves, and the dialogue between masterpieces is, after all, spoken for our ears.

[1] *Situations*, II, p. 243. 'The sense of history flooded over us; in everything that we touched, in the air that we breathed, in the page that we read, in the one that we wrote, in love itself we discovered an undertaste of history, that is, a bitter and ambiguous mingling of the absolute and the transitory.'

They are of course, the only ears possible, and it is doubtful that any critical attitude can be consistently framed that claims otherwise. (Just as it is doubtful that the critics of expressionism can frame a satisfactory aesthetic that is entirely without expressionist elements.) The events of the past may belong to the past and be hidden by time—the objects of the past are with us still, and no real understanding is possible without accepting some interaction between them and ourselves. And this in turn requires an observer who is more than a tabula rasa. Recognition of our own presence of course implies that, in a very minimal sense, historicism is a normal condition of any look to the past, or of any interpretation of the objects the past has left us. The alternative would mean the end of interpretation, and finally the consignment both of events and works to an unapproachable limbo. That we are in some way 'situated' before works of art is inseparable from our humanity—insofar as we have any cognizance of works of art at all—and such a minimal historicism is the consequence of a normal capacity for seeing, and need imply no serious falsification. But then, historical context too may involve our experience and imagination, and corruption through the self is better prevented by taste than by rule, by sense of proportion rather than by doctrine. And Gombrich may have good reason to doubt that such balance and tact will be preserved in a work which is personal and romantic to the point of being visionary, and where aesthetic insight is that of the seer.

5. THE 'SMALL CHANGE' OF THE VISIONARY

The professional consideration of Malraux seems normally to end with a sop thrown to the distinguished man of letters, an acknowledgment of 'the impact of the expressionist crisis' on a 'rich and sensitive mind',[1] or the impression of 'a sensitive, brilliant, troubled mind setting down a wide variety of moving reactions to the power of painting and sculpture'.[2] Once theses and arguments are discarded, the remainder allowed is that acuteness and vividness of personal impression and response that characterize an individual man, a combination of sensibility and intelligence, and in spite of its unsystematic character,

[1] Gombrich, op. cit. [2] Sloane, op. cit.

of great knowledge. In a writer whose method is so personal, whose aim and style are so essentially visionary, we might be concerned only with the unique quality of the way of seeing, as we are with Blake, or alternatively with the way in which critical remarks are a part of the writer's whole message, as we are with D. H. Lawrence. With Malraux the manner and the message are clearly inseparable. The step from time and ordinary context into the Museum unites the critical device with the fact of the vision.

Yet prophets and visionaries are notoriously the most difficult of mankind to take at their face value, their disciples a minority indistinguishable from cranks. Our suspicions alternate from those of wish-fulfilment, self-indulgence and fantasy, to those of an unbearable high-seriousness and the inflation of moral grandeur. To the cold eyed and professional, to the congenital enemy of enthusiasm, Malraux may well share in these follies. But two mitigations must be constantly urged. Unlike those prophets that have railed against moral corruption, or urged mankind to some form of moral action, the aesthetic visionary has no aim but to make men see. Wholly uncramped by doctrine Malraux wishes only to portray the grandeur and importance of art, the sublime qualities of the individual masterpiece, and if he is to restore us to the lost faith in human credentials, to resurrect the fading image of man, he seeks to do so only by showing man's noblest works to what advantage he can.

Furthermore, it is worth emphasizing again how Malraux's method is a development and intensification of a normal and respectable critical practice. All of us use some milder form of 'arrachement' in isolating important or favoured works as subjects of reflection. And most of us, to some extent or other, create an 'Imaginary Museum' in our own minds, a collection of those works that have mattered far more than others. We may well debate the relative status of the various works within it and try to discriminate among personal affections, interests or beliefs that have guided our choice. I. A. Richards has remarked that the responsibility of criticism is in the maintaining of an 'art of choice', an active power of discriminating and choosing among the many styles and standards of the art of the world. It is easy to see, in our age of multiple values, the necessary element of eclecticism in any critical decision. We also, I think, assume a right to take our private 'museum' seriously, to see patterns in our taste that reveal patterns of character, or that suggest the outlines of a 'form of life' which is a personal matter of great consequence. Some critics have felt that this personal pattern of choice is as far as one can go in giving the proper explanations of the ground of critical judgment. Gide remarked in the preface to his anthology of French poetry that he knew better than to make a claim on the taste of the future, and presented his own choice as a reflection of his own age and his own life. And this is a classical historicist point of view.

With respect to the reader's own sensibility, one of the important if double-edged effects of Malraux's 'arrachement' is an assault on entrenched visual and intellectual habits, perhaps even to the point that the shock treatment becomes an end in itself. Because of our normal education to the importance of historical context, we may accept the native affinities of works too easily and uncritically, and even what may pass for the 'imaginary museum' in our mind seldom subjects the works in it to that close comparison that forces us to see them anew. Malraux confronts these habits of mind with an array of new affinities, which need not displace the old, but in suggesting new contexts for the familiar leads to multiple perspectives, an enlarged capacity for re-seeing from a variety of points of view. This may, to some extent, reflect Malraux's delight in agility for its own sake, and could be allowed to degenerate into facile smartness. But the intention behind it is quite serious, a continual widening and complicating of our sensibility. 'Architecture suggests . . . ' of course the familiar: façades, colonnades, forms and surfaces, not the geometrical jungle of Barbadour (M 18–19). To extend our view of what architecture may be is to extend our view of mankind, of its total possibilities and creative powers. The danger here is again what I have suggested, not that sort of eclecticism that through fussiness narrows and impoverishes taste, but that an exuberant universality may swamp the powers of discrimination, and the search for every new form of expressive powers of the imagination is too concerned with objects which have doubtful credentials as works of art.

This was of course Berenson's claim, that such a universality implied the vanishing of standards. Could it not mean simply a greater complexity of standards? There is no theoretical reason why universality and standards are incompatible, although some excursions into marginal arts may obviously pose problems. Judgment on these matters must be a bringing together of many kinds of knowledge, and even then will be uncertain in the face of incompatible historical presuppositions. Judgment must always reside in the sense of the particular case and Malraux's sympathy comprehends an astonishing variety, largely because universality matters to him more than strictness. Generosity and instinctive receptiveness are his natural predisposition. Yet even if Malraux's universal scope is sometimes attained at the expense of a stylistic Tower of Babel, it is quite necessary to his scheme that the whole of mankind with the enormous variety of their expressive traditions should be represented. And here again the difference with Berenson is not a critical difference, but one which reflects a total view of art and of mankind. However isolated and self-limiting it may sometimes appear, the contents and character of the Museum must be judged in terms of an ulterior purpose which embraces more than art.

The freedom that Malraux gains through his universality of scope is that of combining his personal vision of 'Man's Fate' with a vision of world history. The extension of his Museum to the most remote of styles is clearly to avoid a narrow, western European parochialism. In every society and in every age we see the same confrontation of man with his destiny, and in this confrontation a creative response which however monstrous or civilized, becomes a form of 'conquest'. Whatever the visual material it always leads Malraux back to his essential themes using the object of art as a means of exploration and dramatic display, to ring all the possible changes on the uniqueness of the 'only animal who knows he is to die'. The brooding presence of the common fate is as oppressive and insistent in the episodes of the artistic past as in the prison yards of Shanghai, or the isolation of the trapped tank. Sometimes, in fact, this insistence becomes fatiguing, and like fading mementi mori with which we have learned to live, the imminence has vanished, and custom has staled our sense of crisis. At such moments we are less aware of art than of the pressures behind it, and through these pressures the meaning of the phrase 'psychology of art' steadily deepens. Whatever others might wish it to mean, this notion in Malraux turns away from the empirical features of the visual world and the mechanics of the artist's work, to the spiritual forces within the soul of the artist himself.

So what we learn from this psychology is more about men than about objects ('more about artists than about art . . . '),[1] and precisely as the heroes of the novels these are men who live on the heights, images of ourselves fantastically magnified, and shorn of the baggage of the ordinary. Consequently their inner selves become in turn the subject matter of another art, and every detail of their creative lives adds something, another facet or dimension to the greater artifice, man, who becomes under Malraux's hands an artistic construction in his own right. The move from the particular to the general has called forth more than mere abstraction, and to this work of art, as to the creative process behind the museum contents themselves, Malraux brings powers which are essentially rhetorical—powers which profoundly reshape whatever reality they are meant to convey.

Eclecticism, dilettantism, brilliant moments of impressionist evocation, startling but isolated moments of insight, the demolition of convention for the sake of seeing works in a wholly new way—these are the 'small change' of the visionary. It would be impossible to claim that these should substitute for the more solid and meticulous forms of scholarship, but it is possible to find through them another kind of illumination, by way of a romantic sensibility gifted with enormous power of projection and evocation. These are of course quite appropriate if we consider that in Malraux's case the one sort of demonstration is ostensive, where the aim is to evoke the power of revelation intrinsic to art itself. But if such matters are beyond the demonstration of argument, and the powers of suggestion fail to capture us for the visionary message, our imagination may still respond, and may under some circumstances give a more rewarding and even valid experience than that gained through the systematic professional explanations that leave the imagination unengaged.

For this is one sense of 'la critique engagée', and it is central both to such criticism, and to the romantic attitude that so

[1] Sloane, op. cit.

often informs it, depending so profoundly on psychological projection and imaginative identification, that the effects of such criticism should not show themselves in argument or in doctrine, but obliquely, through the various ways in which such commitment involves our sympathies and energies. And in this case Malraux's engagement makes the same sort of claim on us as works of art themselves, demands our involvement as though we were spectators at a tragedy, where one would be insensible to sit unmoved. Indeed, in great measure, Malraux's work is conceived as a tragedy, the tragedy of that curious abstraction Man, except that Malraux seeks through his own rhetorical power to supplant pity and fear with dignity and awe.

III. The Paradox of the Rhetorical Hero

I. RHETORIC AND TRUTH

PICON has suggested that the underlying point of departure for *Les Voix du Silence* is a distinction between an 'art of rhetoric' and an 'art of truth'.[1] In the former it is the artist who counts for more than he has presented; in the latter, art is devoted to its subject matter. This may be an uneasy distinction, but if it is true that the Museum accepts, or even favours an art of rhetoric, in its anxiety to isolate the more expressive gestures of mankind, it is relevant to ask how the same distinction applies to Malraux himself, remembering that in his earliest work it seemed the man behind the page that really mattered, with the work often subordinated to a revelation of the man. It is one of the special talents of Malraux that he can project himself into a character or situation with unsurpassed intensity, and yet leave behind the impression that the man is somehow more than the work. In some writers, like D. H. Lawrence, a similar ambiguity and shifting of interest between the legend and the printed page is enforced by a pervasive didacticism. The man is both prophet and teacher; the works are not self-contained, but are fragments of a revelation to be understood only in terms of the total message. That this is not Malraux's intention, in his novels at least, is made clear in his famous reply to Trotsky's critique of the political attitudes of the revolutionaries in *Les Conquérants*. He was creating a work of art, not a political treatise. And the major novels, *La Condition*

[1] Picon, op. cit., p. 99.

68

Humaine and *L'Espoir* are works that seem completely self-contained, that display human character for its own sake, not as the illustration of doctrine.

Yet in the mixture of life and art, in patterns visible through the development of successive heroes, in the diffusion of interest among fictional episodes and those in the life of the author, there is a continuum whose elements would be difficult to divide. The interaction of man and art is of such complexity that it might be impossible to devise a serious case where the distinction between a pure 'art of rhetoric' and an 'art of truth' could be maintained. However, Picon's suggestion about the importance of an 'art of rhetoric' may illuminate two of the most important features of Malraux's aesthetic. One is the extent to which the works themselves must be seen as rhetorical structures, and reflect a rhetorical use of language. Caught up in the hypnosis of their own joy in persuasion, they are themselves symbolic gestures whose claims are those of art, not of argument. The other is the extent to which, as I have already mentioned, the discussion of art ends in talk of the artist, of the spiritual force of his creative action. The drama of man's triumph over his destiny is the drama of creativity, where the observation of the finished work should be subordinate to the human action of which it forms the most significant part. The uncertainty as to whether Malraux's own books should be called works of art or critical commentary might only confuse the issue. The giving of such names is not always of the greatest importance, and the works are none the worse for defying the conventional division into genres. If critical works arise from the same problems as the novels, they also allow themselves the same freedom of invention. Hence an indifference to ordinary logic, or perhaps the reliance on logic of another kind: ' . . . rituels, conventionnels ou banals, ses gestes font appel à une logique' (218).[1]

To some such logic Malraux himself appeals. The completion of almost any step in Malraux's progress is not to be found in the drawing of a rationalized conclusion, but in identification with a moment of rhetorical intensity; the truth to be established is somehow bound up with the language that establishes it. The style of *Les Voix du Silence* is consciously elevated and vatic,

[1] ' . . . rituals, conventional or banal, its gestures appeal to a logic of their own.'

69

an inspired proclamation, quite unabashed by its own preten-
sions, or the variety of rhetorical equipment used. Several
stylistic devices are of special importance, two of them consistent features of Malraux's method of comparison: the *startling
connection* and the *mysterious ellipsis*. The former is designed to
force the mind into movement, to connect the familiar with the
remote, the West with the East, the primitive with the sophis-
ticated, and all with the modern. The latter is a simple suppres-
sion of the steps by which such connections might be shown, of
relying on the imaginative impact of suggestion, rather than the
careful tracing of the relation of one detail to another. And as
a complement to these two one should probably add the *unspoken
implication*, the leaving of a series of suggestions to complete
itself, once the imaginative train of reflection is under way.

Furthermore, the connections are seldom simple, and it is
almost never a single leap of the imagination that is required,
but a series of them, the series becoming easily a lengthy com-
pilation of parallel cases ranged side by side. So the comparison
becomes a list, a flow of proper names, each evoking a complex
of associations—and an enormous range of them may be devoted
to the illustration of what may be a very simple idea. Almost
chosen at random a single paragraph may contain the names:
Renoir, Chartres, Giotto, Reims, Bamberg, Naumberg, Senlis,
Mantes, Laon, Goya, Bayeu, Manet, Michelangelo, Donatello,
Rembrandt, Lastmann, Elsheimer, El Greco, Bassano, Piero
della Francesca—and several of them repeated (306). All of
these are used in illustration of the problem of giving sense to
the notion of copying. A problem which is interesting enough,
but the examples are not used to give unique light that the individual case can shed on such a notion. Rather than a series
of careful and distinct discriminations, differentiated by specific
qualities, the examples are merely lumped together, arrayed to
give an observation a look of massive support—in effect, to
overwhelm.

I do not mean that the examples are misleading or that as
individual cases they are not in some way connected with the
general drift of Malraux's intention, only that as specific cases
they seem to have no separate life or individual function. They
are rather the fragments of a train of association, and the overall
effect of the ensemble is cumulative, with each particular

adding weight to the whole. The same pattern is seen in Malraux's description of how fundamentally 'apart' the masterpiece is from the total *œuvre* of a painter, where he invokes the 'Mona Lisa', Rembrandt's 'Three Crosses' and 'Prodigal Son', Vermeer's 'Love Letter', a Titian Pietà, The Kings of Chartres, the Villeneuve Pietà, the 'Embarkation for Cythère' and 'Enseignement de Gersaint', 'Hélène Fourment' and 'Philopoemen', Vermeer's 'Young Lady with Turban' and 'View of Delft', 'The Madonna of the Chair' and the 'School of Athens', Van der Weyden's portraits, his 'Annunciation' and 'Descent from the Cross', two works of Fouquet, Giotto, the Arezzo frescos and Piero's London 'Nativity' (453). The argument is that masterpieces do not imply one another as the common run of a painter's works may do, but leap out of context to create a scale of values of their own. But this is merely asserted and then repeated, never qualified for the individual case or developed; the aim is to gain intensity and depth as the succession of names becomes somehow a landslide of insight. Again, the cases referred to are not in any way considered and the point to be established is treated as self-evident, with every example a magical key to another dimension of inescapable truth. The lists become a litany, an incantation indeed, and take on a specific quality of religious utterance, that of ritual repetition. Yet without the conventionalism that this often implies, for the litany is charged with feeling, enthusiasm, with impassioned belief. And it seems intended not only to overwhelm but to amaze. The ideal reader is perhaps one who only haltingly follows, alternatively astonished by the imagination's dazzling flight, and reassured by the wholesale reference. The effect of the reference in the mass should be like reading shorthand, with each allusion as it flashes by releasing its appropriate range of connotations.

Rhetorical reinforcement to some extent consists of gymnastic paths to old truths, and where the conclusion is to be reached by accumulation, it is still sometimes left for the reader himself to draw the moral; or at other moments the whole of the argument may hang on a single noun or adjective, arriving dramatically at the end of a sentence to give focus and purpose to what has gone before. Single words too have their special magic, and throughout these books certain key terms gather special meanings and connotations of their own. Some

F   71

expressions: 'l'Eternel', 'conquête', 'métamorphose', 'triomphe', 'destin', 'apparence', 'l'Absolu', and above all 'l'Homme', are repeated in an incantatory style which produces an atmosphere of rhetorical intoxication, almost of mystery. One can see from the stylistic heightening alone that this is nothing at all in the way of a descriptive treatise where the terms have normal denotative meanings. One is the presence of a language where the obscure echoes and overtones are the most important thing about it, and it sometimes seems that Malraux wishes to elevate the imaginative margins of language into the appropriate medium of prophecy, and even to create the divinity of man through sheer verbal conjury.

Whether or not this is his real intention, it is certainly suggested in his verbal effect and this rhetorical creation points to the contradictory or paradoxical character of the whole work. To create a religion of the values revealed through art would require some force beyond that of ordinary persuasion. That these magic words should in an individual and highly charged way attempt to become the special vehicle of revelation is understandable enough. The verbal conjury is the attempt to create a faith, or rather to make worthy of ecstatic devotion the very ambiguous fact of man's presence to which art gives a transformation. In doing so Malraux wishes to give tragic dimensions to ordinary human destiny, and without sentimentalizing the fate of 'everyman'. The words used must suggest many ranges of metaphysical meanings, and yet commit themselves to none. The traditional languages of metaphysics and theology, for all of their obscurity, still have postulated meanings about the order of things. But these words of Malraux in spite of their direct address to our situations seem to exist in an order of their own like the works of art in the Museum they purport to describe or reflect, whose dialogue may be intended for our ears, but whose collective presence suggests a disturbing self-containment. In Malraux's rhetorical creation words share the isolation of their subject matter, and seem governed by rules of their own making, invoking in themselves as through works of art an existential Pantheon of self-created gods. Through double means this rhetorical hero creates an existential humanism on aesthetic grounds.

As the essential terms of this are left to their penumbral

selves, the real implications and commitments are never articulated. Malraux instead returns in case after case to what he regards as the fundamentals of the human situation: the capacity to comment is the fact of being man, and the exploitation of that comment the act of revolt against destiny. The revolt of man underlies the act of the artist as it did that of the terrorist in *La Condition Humaine*. The response to the absurdity of the human condition is to create forms 'powerful enough' to deny it, a creation that is a more profound because more eloquent form of 'testimony' than the act of irrational violence. But what kind of 'power' is involved in such images, and what does the artist actually accomplish through it? His images that deny man's Fate in no way alter it—the facts of death and time remain as before. It is an ambiguous triumph to deny the consequences of an absurdity which still exists. Yet if the 'rhetorical creation' in no way alters the facts of the real creation, it may still alter the character of man's place within it. The artist's rejection or transcendence of the absurd is also his escape from the obsession with death that consumes Tchen. Unlike the Sisyphus of Camus whose happiness is in the head-on confrontation with the fact of the absurd, the artist's gesture in effect denies the weight of the stone in the same moment that the fact of being an artist accepts it. The absurdity of fate is the springboard to an art which must deny it. 'Mais il est artiste,' Malraux says of Goya, 'et ce sentiment devient par cà irréductible à l'absurde . . . ' (S/155).[1]

While something may be implicit about a 'metaphysics of art', Malraux's existentialism is quite unconcerned with its place in any traditional metaphysical scheme, something for which it has been seriously criticized. This is partly because Malraux has so thoroughly dramatized something from which in the end he has shied away. The temptation of the 'Absolute' runs through his work, and Malraux is so acutely aware of what metaphysical absolutes have meant to men in the past that a positive nostalgia emanates from those pages devoted to an age of faith, a nostalgia apparent in calling a crucifix by Giotto a testament, Leonardo's 'Last Supper' a 'sublime anecdote'. The powerful spell of the former is all too obvious. Testaments signify in a way that anecdotes do not, and when Malraux

[1] 'But he is an artist, and his thought is for that reason irreducible to the absurd.'

speaks of man's art as a testament he seems to reach for an analogue which is never complete, to find testimony without a certainty as to its end. Yet it is less than relevant to point out that Malraux's humanism is metaphysically inadequate, that the artist's defence against destiny is no substitute for the Kingdom of Heaven. Malraux produces no metaphysical solutions to a problem which by its formulation seems to exclude them; his is an existential stance, not a metaphysical platform, a style or attitude, not a doctrine. And the insistence on a clear conceptual stand would both be an insistence on an act of dishonesty on Malraux's part, as well as a misunderstanding of his own relation to his subject matter. Not a speculative philosopher seeking abstract explanations, he is above all a witness to the common human tragedy, an observer immersed in the particulars of man's groping with an eternal dilemma.

Between God and nothingness there exists the simple fact of man's presence in the world—something which gives us the empirical ground of reflection. Art, says Malraux, is testimony. But of what? We have the human presence to account for. Yet God has existed, for we see his presence in the testimony of the past? Or is it that man has created him? Malraux does not try to decide—his own response so far as it can be formulated, seems empirical, sceptical, fatalistic. His particular gift is that of giving dramatic intensity to the facts of the human situation, and of showing the impact of that situation on what we can see of man's nature and creative powers. He is above all the spiritual chronicler of the human revolt, and his also is the artist's double rôle of actor and commentator. For him, the fact of man's presence and dignity can only be given a dramatic instantiation, a *picture* of that presence with its many resonances, but not a rationalization. By creating his own values what does man create? By asserting his humanity against the void what does he assert? These questions remain to trouble Malraux—as to trouble any form of humanism. But perhaps the most specific and immediate contribution of existentialist humanism, and of Malraux's in particular, is to give us a more profound and dramatic sense of human reality in the face of the void.

One or two qualifications are suggested by the marked shift in emphasis in the three successive versions of the aesthetic works. In the latest, and unfinished incarnation, *La Méta-*

morphose des Dieux, which is actually a second re-writing of what we should consider as a single work, the faces of the gods are more conspicuously in view. Here Malraux focuses more directly on their image, follows more closely and chronologically their development in the human mind. The interplay of the divine and the human is given a more careful and schematic framework. To a large extent the purpose seems to be to clarify and organize the chaotic materials of the earlier versions, a care which brings the work closer in spirit to more conventional academic works. In some ways this is not an advantage: the original form, *La Psychologie de l'Art*, was a series of disjointed insights, of tentative and often brilliant gropings, which relied on the extraordinary effect of individual details. The gradual ordering through successive re-writings has lessened its freshness, and order has been attained at the expense of the direct feeling for the works in question. The increasing trouble taken to rationalize the structure of the whole seems to push a work whose greatest appeal is in the immediacy of its eloquence towards an academic standard, by which it will inevitably be inferior to conventional academic works.

Perhaps the increased emphasis on the gods is only the accident of a tightened chronology which causes the first volume of *La Métamorphose des Dieux* to deal with largely religious art. But the quality of reverence seems also to have grown, the faces of the gods are scanned more keenly than ever, the atmosphere of religious celebration is more marked than before. How intentional this is and what it signifies we must wait to see. Although Malraux has absorbed and exemplified the Nietzschean attitude, where the death of God is accepted as a challenge, as a stage-setting for the heroic existence of man, the obsessive return to the faces of the gods suggests an excitement in something more than the imaginative power that has 'created' them. But to turn an 'art of rhetoric' into an 'art of truth' would be to step beyond art itself.

2. AESTHETIC HUMANISM

If man is the rhetorical hero, and it is by the power of expression that he becomes himself, Malraux's humanism is based on a highly personal and intensified form of a concept at least as old as Aristotle's notion of the superiority of the contemplative man. It was a commonplace of the ancient world that reflective intelligence based on the power of speech, the fact of self-awareness and the power of expressing it distinguished the human creature and ennobled him, and gave him the closest thing to kinship with the gods. However, there is nothing in Malraux which suggests either the neatness or the assured rationalism of ancient psychology. The whole background of Malraux is overwhelmingly romantic, and he shares the romantic presupposition of a human self, infinite in its capacities and creative powers, and capable of incalculable transformation through the will. The heroism of man, as it was for Nietzsche, is the fulfilment of a will. In Malraux's career, the will has taken two forms: the *political will*, whose essential features are commitment and action, and the *rhetorical will* devoted to an indirect creation through the powers of human expression. And of course it is a short psychological step from 'willing' to 'choosing', the essential existential act.

In *Les Voix du Silence* the notion of choice takes two natural forms: the selectivity of the artist's eye and brush, and the discrimination of the connoisseur. The former is the more significant series of assertions and excisions, and Malraux gives us a passionate and delicate account of what in some sense we may have always known but never wholly realized, of the artist's creativity. To choose means also to reject, and part of the artist's creating of new worlds is his refusal of others. So the great masters, Michelangelo, Goya, Manet, turned their backs on surroundings and conventions to step into a visual world of their own. And the fact of such choice even extends to the physical details of the artist's labour—the famous slow-motion film of Matisse painting startled the master himself. He had no idea how many tentative movements he had rejected.

With the choices involved in the case of appreciation one might possibly doubt their definitive and decisive nature. The choices are not by their nature absolutely exclusive, for we can in theory appreciate every sort of art, and objects on every imaginable level of success or failure, seeing in the endless gradations of one's judgment an aesthete's version of 'the great chain of being'. But such a taste would reflect a formlessness and neutrality of self as foreign to Malraux as the detachment of pure scholarship—and for much the same reason. The self would abdicate before the work. Appreciation for Malraux is a form of action. To choose a work or a style is to some extent to choose a self, to identify, at least in the imagination, with a 'form of life' which has consequences for one's whole being.

Consequently there is a sense in which the 'art of choice' reflects a far-reaching view of human personality, where the very notion of man involves choices and decisions, where character is almost constructed in eclectic fashion out of an heterogeneous sprinkling of qualities and talents. Having no viable tradition, 'no faith, no beliefs or ideology . . . ' modern man must assemble an image of himself out of the materials available, and in an age of crisis which has put so much of the human past in doubt, this involves a careful choosing among the elements of human accomplishment. The *self*, in effect, is a small model of the Museum, carefully chosen according to principles which cannot avoid the aesthetic. It is Malraux's and the existentialist belief that all values must be created whole cloth out of one's natural resources and from the will—in his case perhaps, a 'volonté farouche'. To have an identity is to choose an identity, and by choosing to create one. But the existentialist is also limited by history, however optimistic his belief in human plasticity. In action as in art the only models are those that other men have left us, and to go beyond them is still to go by way of them. The necessity for balance and proportion, the movement toward 'harmony in strength' makes the aesthetic element in such a composition of the self obvious enough, and connects Malraux with older traditions of humanism, with the *kalos kagathos* of ancient Athens, or that Renaissance image of man as a work of art, so dear to Burkhardt and Nietzsche, and whose supreme exemplars were so often artists: Leonardo and Michelangelo, or Leon Battista Alberti.

Beyond this association with more traditional humanism lies something perhaps Faustian and more magical. The most suspect element in Malraux has always been the 'fascinateur' or 'prestidigitateur'—the magical but meretricious juggler of glittering words, striving for a spell, producing a panoply of effects without certainty of substance. That Malraux recognizes this dimension of his own talent seems clear from the 'shaman' passage in *Les Noyers de l'Altenburg*. And for him there may well be some profound connection between the importance of the created thing and the depth of mystery that surrounds it. With the chosen heroes among the greatest artists, this is produced by a kind of hypothetical psychology which reaches into their inner life, and somehow 'explains' while exalting the mystery. And with respect to Malraux himself the combination of mystery and dazzle has suggested to some a certain falsity of tone along with an inflated sense of personal grandeur. But the false tone is in some sense inevitable when the whole concept of self is governed by the will. The self is an artifice insofar as it is 'chosen', and the Museum that resembles it cannot escape in its composition the arbitrariness of the will.

But what further character can one give to the will which shapes the foundation of Malraux's humanism? Guided by an aesthetic of heightened moments, of 'extreme situations' and stunning occasions of visual recognition, it is above all *rhetorical*, concerned to alter the condition of man by the power of words, and to raise a humanistic assertion to the level of religion by that same power. One is not, however, obliged to ask if the 'leap' to faith can be accomplished through rhetoric—for the only faith demanded is a faith in the power of the word itself. Malraux's humanism is established by mere assertion and asks us only to believe in the fact of the assertion—in the eloquent voice in the wilderness that proclaims in the name of mankind, 'Here I am.'

This may take on a manner which rings with intolerable egoism; it may be an assertion for the sake of the gesture and so without consequences; or it may in the end be a humanism which partakes of that hollowness which we sometimes associate with the notion of rhetoric. But there is, in Malraux's own terms, a confrontation of man with his fate that is something matter-of-fact and profoundly honest, both dreadful and pathetic. The exaltation of man does not lessen the tragedy of man, it deepens it—the greater the creature the more monstrous the fact of his fall. The Nietzschean and existentialist stance that encounters nothingness is dramatized rather than obscured by a flood of language which tries to convert self-assertion into a hymn of triumph.

3. RHETORIC AND TRAGEDY

Malraux has no doubt that the proper successor of gods and heroes is the artist, and in this recurrent claim it is easy to trace two of the artist's persistent features. The artist is the natural successor of the gods in respect to creativity—the maker of a private world ex-nihilo, and the natural successor of the heroes of action as the leaders of man's revolt, so he embodies the roles of both Zeus and Prometheus. In this duality the artist in *Les Voix du Silence* parts company with the many fashionable artist-heroes of modern literature. They may share the same isolation, the necessity for detachment and the inevitability of suffering, but Malraux's artist hero is never the man of sensibility, the passive reflector and observer, making the refined discrim-inations of his counterparts in James or Thomas Mann. The artist hero of modern literature is essentially passive; while his sensibilities may sound the depths of experience, and respond to those nuances of human feeling that are ignored by a harsh mechanical world, and he may speak with a richness of under-standing denied to the ordinary man, his artistic gifts are simply the pre-condition of being the sort of man he is. We are seldom convinced of anything that concerns the character of his art in its own right.

In Aschenbach and the Jamesian artists, the fact of being an artist is only the backdrop for the appreciation of some quality of experience that is to follow. And Gide's *Faux-Monnayeurs* contains an explicit critique of this image of the artist's charac-ter, focusing in Edouard on the impossibility of moving from this passivity of sensibility to the act of creation. It is rarely, above all in Proust—and possibly in *Doctor Faustus*—that we feel any of the reality of a character's creative powers in action. But then, novels deal with the relation of persons to circum-stance, and for Malraux the beginning of creative power is in the capacity to transcend circumstance. And this transcendence makes the artist the culture hero of civilization. It is the artist who has undertaken the deepest exploration of life, but has also the power to express his understanding of it, to give it form, and in doing so to remake the civilization of which it is a part. As a culture hero he is the representative of other men, the one who has taken on himself most wholly the human prerogative of self-assertion. The artist for Malraux is not the sensibility but the *will* of mankind.

Whether or not the consummation of this will is in objects of art, the study of it is in the inner lives of men, and to a great extent the 'psychology of art' becomes a specialized form of biography. Studies of painters become essays in hypothetical psychology, capturing by an extravagant sympathy hundreds of imaginary details of the creative response. We are taken into the inner chamber of the artist's mind, have a 'privileged access' perhaps unavailable to the artist himself. This operates above all with those artists like Van Gogh and Goya, Michelangelo and Rembrandt where an artistic evolution is accompanied by manifest signs of spiritual conflict. The aim is to catch the inner moment of creativity, the firing point of the creative act. It is perhaps this 'privileged access' which seems most wholly irresponsible to the art historian; the revelations are quite impossible either to confirm or refute. These hypothetical descriptions can claim to no certain knowledge of any kind, and are themselves a work of imaginative projection, a fiction devised by one artist to represent the inner workings of others. Such a projection enables Malraux to play the dilettante among psyches as well as among works of art, moving with grace and facility from one to another version of the human predicament, from the private torments of Van Gogh to the pious intensities of the Romanesque.

Through all of these inner studies, however, the fact seems to remain constant that the capacity to cry out against destiny matters more than the structure of syllables in the cry—whatever forms man happens to create have the equivalent function of revealing Man. The object of art is like an optical instrument, or like one of those miraculous devices of modern medicine that is especially adapted to the inner view, and can somehow capture its significant outlines. But the question always remains to trouble Malraux as to how the inner view is significant. Certainly in the one respect that Malraux so fervently repeats, the visible fact of an inner outline, of the presence of form implicit in our very humanity is the basis of significance, and the multiplicity of such forms the ostensive demonstration of the richness and resource of humanity.

But as creators the great masters are set apart, and this is an ambiguity Malraux never explains or seeks to resolve. They are both the representatives of a 'Man' so abstract that he cannot but embrace the whole. Yet insofar as they are set apart there cannot help but be another dimension to their humanity, and even the fact of perceiving the masterpiece separates an individual from the mass of humanity; in exercising his consciousness he also undergoes a transformation, the knowledge and love of the masterpiece means again a dimension to the self, and masterpieces are not for everybody. 'Il y a un roman des masses, pas de Stendhal des masses; une musique des masses, pas de Bach—ni de Beethoven, quoi qu'on en dise; une peinture des masses, pas de Piero della Francesca, ni de Michel-Ange' (512).[1] Both creation and perception are for the individual, and imply a power which rescues him from the humdrum and banal, which require not only innate powers, but refinement and discipline. Through the object of art the creator finds himself and the art-lover sees himself, enlarged and set apart, enabled both to find a sense of identity, and a semblance of perspective on the chaos of things.

The fact of this power and the added reality which genius and the understanding of it give to human life provides Malraux with the ground of his notion of the relation of the personal to the historical self. The artist like the shaman has a special kind of identity, almost an analogous power of 'translocation'. Through the creative act he is released from personal history into 'History'. The entry into the Museum is both the apotheosis and the transcendence of the personal. This is partially analogous to the political submergence of the personal in the novels. In dying for his cause Kyo seems to transcend his personal fate, and to identify himself through action with some essential pattern of things. The official ideology of *La Condition Humaine* affirms that action and sacrifice may project one out of oneself (although I have suggested that the novel as a whole may not entirely support this official line), that the self should be lost in the name of a greater cause, that the corn of wheat should die, the individual be submerged in what is greater than himself—even when for Malraux this was not the denial of the uniqueness and import-

[1] 'There is a novel for the masses, but no Stendhal for the masses; a music for the masses, but no Bach—nor Beethoven, whatever one may say; a painting for the masses, but no Piero della Francesca nor Michelangelo.'

ance of the particular human creature. However, an antithetical vision remorselessly pursues any such doctrine, and this is an emphasis on the simple fact of human passion and suffering, and the discovery in them of something greater than the march of events—as the sense of the flesh 'encore vivante' effaces history for Hernandez, or the song of the mad Nietzsche in the darkness of the railway carriage 'effaced the dark itself'. There are in effect two versions of romantic individualism in Malraux, and he seems concerned to accommodate both of them to his views of art and of history. One comprehends the meaning of annihilation and sacrifice; the submission to 'otherness' has its romantic grandeur. The other is the moment of self-assertion when the individual identifies itself through form. And the double nature of works of art reaches out towards both, capturing on the one hand the individual moment of feeling or perception, yet on the other removing it from the normal human frame, into the otherness of history embodied in the timeless Museum.

This should in principle effect the reconciling of a conflict—Malraux is always torn between the eternal and the moment, the absolute and the transitory—but the cost of such reconciliation is seen in the way in which the isolation of the Museum subtly alters the character of its contents. I have pointed out the essential rôle of isolation in creating the aesthetic attitude, of the capacity to stand off from experience in order to recapture it —the essential condition of the creation of art as well as its appreciation. And this applies to Malraux in his own double rôle of artist and commentator or one might better say that his work as artist and critic are inseparable, proceeding from the same impulses and presuppositions, employing the same talents. In turn, Malraux's involvement with the inner lives of artists is indistinguishable from his involvement with pictures, and the inner workings of artists compose themselves into aesthetic elements, the psychological version of the picturesque. Action, creation, expression are dissolved into one another, caught up in the Museum's dialectic of involvement and detachment, often frozen together in the same rhetorical cliché, or carried by the same rhetorical élan.

Yet if the act of expression is the act of heroism, this has a curious corollary. Professor Levin has remarked that 'André Malraux . . . has been journeying across the world, searching for adventures large enough to exalt the modern intellectual into a tragic hero'.[1] 'Intellectual', not 'artist'. It is precisely the intellectual's personal tragedy that he does query where he cannot answer, discover where he cannot explain, and perceive where he cannot act. The artist stands for him in the world of forms as a substitute creator, inventing images of those perplexities and harmonies, torments and delights that make up his situation. Yet it is inevitably a substitution, and the tragedy of Malraux is in the eternal incapacity of such a substitution to attain the real. True, in Nietzsche's maxim the artist rejects and defies reality. But this in effect commits him to the tragic view. And both as a maker and observer Malraux seems, more than the artists he describes, to be a rhetorical Sisyphus, frenziedly pushing the works of mankind to an unattainable height where they would be more than the works of mankind. Whatever sort of tragic heroism is appropriate to the modern intellectual, the tragedy of Malraux is the tragedy of the will.

As we examine the legendary versions of the struggle of mankind against its destiny, whether a god-haunted destiny or that of the void, there are mythological figures enough for the many forms that the visual imagination has captured. The play among objects of art has provided Malraux with endless mythological resource to satisfy the love of richness in detail which animates throughout his work the surface excitement of his language. Rather than a 'temple dedicated to a myth' his Museum is a meeting place of many, even of incompatible myths, the display case for any myth whatsoever that gives form and identity to human experience. But it is impossible to say that the many tensions of this rich surface are harmonized, or the fundamental incompatibilities intelligibly resolved. Prometheus and Saturn are uneasily encompassed; Apollo and Baluba 'ancestors' receive equivalent welcome. But this assemblage of all myths, of all the forms that seem expressive, poses an awkward dilemma. For the fact of universal acceptance contradicts the possibility of a concrete metaphysical message. If one were to find a metaphysical purpose to the Museum, and it were to have the sort of universal claim which such doctrines traditionally have, one could hardly accept the all-inclusiveness. A religion of art founded on such principles

[1] H. Levin, *James Joyce*, Norfolk, Conn., 1941, p. 211.

would be a religion in name only, and a metaphorical extension of a name at that, for to deify upon an equal ground all the works of mankind, however diverse and contradictory their meaning, is to deny much of their real content and inner character.

Here in effect is a choice that the Museum has evaded, and with good reason. With Malraux's scepticism, his fundamental assumption of man's lonely presence set against its fate, there could be no acceptable ground for the beliefs implicit in any one work of art as opposed to another; whatever the temptations of the absolute there could be no possible ground for choosing among its many forms. However, the alternative emptiness is intolerable to someone of Malraux's personal temperament, so the language of *Les Voix du Silence* devotes its multiple energies to persuade us that its humanism of pure expression is adequate and proper satisfaction to the normal human desire to know where one stands. But the fever of the language itself suggests not conviction but the will to convince—and to be convinced. Rather than resolution there is a perpetual irresolution, with the 'volonté farouche' paralysed in mid-course by the inability either to achieve an end or to renounce the seeking of it.

Yet one could hardly call this state of inner uncertainty, this poised and anxious irresolution a state which is in any way balanced, or reaching towards equilibrium. Rather the Museum is institutionalized paradox, where the fact of a quest that can never succeed becomes a special version of success. It seeks to give to a state of unending striving and ungovernable stress a sort of clean well lighted place, where the gesture is enshrined if its significance is forever unknown, an endless movement arrested in an eternal silence.

But a state of stress, of continuous tension cannot be perpetuated without cost. The Museum involves a strange mixture of rhetorical intensity and underground resignation. One effect of the rhetorical energy in the display of the world's art is that it begins by intoxicating and ends by fatiguing—like a parade that has gone on too long, its trumpet fanfare become monotonous and shrill. With the excitatory rhetoric so prolonged, the conjoining of the remote and exotic under great emotional pressure becomes more blurring than revealing. The air of exaltation, the heightening of style tend to treat the most banal

and the most fantastic, the most recessive and the most demand-
ing works in exactly the same tone. So every nuance of distinction is in the end obscured by the levelling action of a style that
was designed for the opposite purpose.

This fatigue may proceed from something far more than an
over-exposure to a heightened style. It is perhaps rather that
the pure presence of art, the expressive gesture isolated for its
own sake, may be a curiously abstract ground for that vision of
humanity which the Museum is intended to house. A concentration on the expressive, the gestural, the stylistic contour, has
somehow subtly dehumanized the works themselves. Malraux's
critics may have this measure of justice, that their instinctive
response to the isolation of the Museum is sounder than the
academic kinds of reason they have given.[1] Moved from their
context in human action and belief, suddenly confronted with
their remotest peers and ancestors, bizarrely lighted, broken
into fragments to discover the significant detail, they are for a
moment brilliant and provoking, but in the end paler, more
abstract versions of their former selves. The quasi-organic unity
of the 'kingdom of styles' reminds M. Merleau-Ponty of its
Hegelian ancestor, its historicism the equivalent to the manner
in which all philosophies were assimilated and rationalized:
'Hegel, c'est le Musée, c'est toutes les philosophies, si l'on veut,
mais privées de leur finitude et de leur puissance d'impact,
embaumées.'[2] Styles, like philosophies, derive much of their
strength from their rich interaction with the world of which
they are a part. Shorn of this, 'museumed', 'embaumées' if one
will, they somehow fade and diminish. In the Imaginary
Museum conquests have become collector's items.

Analogous in its effect to this detachment of pure expression
is the self-containedness of artistic standards. That modern art
should be a liberation from external values, a concentrating on
what is wholly unique to the nature of art—with formal values
that are entirely an internal matter—may have consequences of
the same order. Deprived of any connection with the world

---

[1] I think it will be clear from the following pages that my criticism of the isolation of the Imaginary Museum is concerned with quite different issues from those
of historical knowledge (Gombrich) or the psychology of perception and creation
(Merleau-Ponty), but is directed to the rôle of art in our experience as a whole.

[2] Merleau-Ponty, op. cit. 'Hegel, there is the Museum, it is all philosophies, if
one wishes, but deprived of their finitude and power of impact, embalmed.'

outside itself, devoted to the play of colour, texture and line, modern art is dehumanized as Ortega y Gasset has said, in turning its back both on the tradition of the human form, or on any connection between its own constructions and the observable features of the life of man. So perhaps an appropriate variation on Malraux's query concerning the 'death of man' would involve asking what kind of life is preserved in a kingdom of styles that has no frame of reference beyond itself. Such an art has become exclusive and mandarin, accepting its isolation for the sake of its freedom. Malraux has set out his visual testimony to reassure himself that man is not dead, that his culture has a continuity, and that his presence in the universe is a matter of consequence. But how far does the self-imposed isolation of the testimony conflict with the intended conclusion, and show us instead something abstract and bloodless, with a lack of conviction in its own presence concealed by feverish rhetoric? Cut off by conditions of their own establishment, may not those conquests by means of forms, those arraignments of the world order by the artist's vision, be themselves bypassed by the course of events, and become nothing more than the exotic possession of another sort of academy, a curious anachronism cultivated by a precious minority, ignored and swallowed up in a mass culture?

Malraux has of course made a doctrine of the alternative: through its newly discovered printing press the world of forms can reach the remote millions, and the creative mission of each masterpiece can touch the remotest sensibility. This is, as his whole work demands, an optimistic vision. The danger, as Professor Wind has recently suggested, is that these forms may be as empty as they are widespread, with the uncomprehended works of the great creators reduced to the status of magazine advertisements, or decorations for the match boxes and coffee tables of the unregarding. The vitality of forms depends not on their distribution, but on the realization that some experience is possible through their presence. And their rôle in Malraux's Museum suggests a more esoteric fate. Their dialogue may be intended for our ears, but ours is an 'over-hearing' that sometimes seems to grasp uneasily the mysterious and internal relations created between the works themselves—relations audible to only the skilled and devoted ear.

Perhaps the place of art in the future is more precarious than

Malraux would allow, and beyond his Museum may lie a state in which standards are so uncertain and diffuse, where human desires and pleasures are so many and so vague, that it is possible that art too may lose its boundaries and identity, and that the supreme expressive power of mankind that Malraux has been at such pains to dramatize may be reduced to a meaningless trifle in a conventionalized and indifferent world. Written to synthesize a view of culture and history, to proclaim its value, exalt its greatness, defend it against dullness, barbarism and ignorance, *Les Voix du Silence* may also be a symptom of its decline, may betray by its anxieties the uncertainties of its end, and reveal its own sense of isolation in the moment of its avowed engagement.

But the sense of personal tragedy is perhaps more immediate than the discovery that the contents of the Museum may themselves belong to the world of the evanescent and transitory. There is still pain in the realization that the most committed of novelists finds the logical consequence of his rôle in the detachment of the spectator in a Museum of his own creating. His whole career would seem reduced to the simple formula: action = art = museum pieces. By what logic has the aesthetic attitude enforced the progressive isolation of the self? And to what extent has the original common struggle, or the fraternal embrace, vanished into that chilly abstraction 'Man'?

It is in terms of this chill, reminiscent of museums themselves, and in spite of the contrasting bouts of rhetorical fever, that the metamorphosis of Malraux seems definitive. While it is true, as late as *Les Noyers de l'Altenburg*, that there are scenes (the gas, the tank, the peasant couple) that dramatize the sense of the human community, they are far from dominating the book. There the true relation of man to his world is in the isolated consciousness uneasily contemplating the whole, and the moments of human contact seem the fitful products of circumstance, almost startling because somehow unreal. Perhaps the long promised sequel, *La Lutte avec l'Ange* will shed more light on this. After *La Psychologie de l'Art* the domination of anxious detachment is only offset by the rhetorical fervour of celebration, and this outlines the tragedy of a will which would deny any fixed distance between vision and reality, and which gives itself with intensity to the effort to turn rhetorical gesture into metaphysical leap—like Zeno's frenzied Achilles pursuing a tortoise Time. For Malraux it is a personal tragedy where the gap between the eternal and the evanescent, the 'absolute and the transitory' cannot be overleaped by faith or conceptual invention, nor by however splendid a construction of the human imagination. Valéry's Socrates suggests both the seductive power and inherent paradox of the rhetorical creation: 'The powers of the soul, as you know come strangely out of the night. . . . By force of illusion they advance to the very borders of the real.' But the borders are never crossed, and between the evanescent and the eternal Malraux's Museum has created not a bridge, but a half-way house.

I have denied the total hermeticism of the museum, and suggested that the importance of the full range of connections of objects of art is known well enough to Malraux. But the greater the understanding the greater the hurt of sacrifice. Works of art may be diminished in what they are if no longer valued for what they were—and yet must escape the corporeal claims of the world to which they once belonged. What the Museum by its very nature would reduce to abstraction Malraux's historical imagination gives life and detail. He more than any of his critics is fully possessed of the variety and complexity of the great masterpieces, with the relevant features of their original context in belief, social order, suffering or pleasure, that wide range of properties both human and formal that make it, among other things, universal. He is the first to protest against the museum chill, and to violate the requirements of a pure kingdom of styles. The sense of isolation I have described may be necessarily implicit in much that he has set before us, but any denial of the rich life and variety of things is contrary to the inclination of the man.

There are two spirits within the museum, one devoted to the isolation of the object of art, to abstraction, to the purity of the expressive moment. The other exults in the detail and variety of all it sees. And this latter has its own form of triumph in the construction of Malraux's aesthetic works. Rather than monolithic they are scattered, rather than direct and linear in their argument they are devious and many sided. These are imaginative works, sometimes closer to prose poems than to essays, or at others a journal of historical marginalia—more inclusive in their sympathies than are the persuasions they entertain. They are richly decorative pieces where the evocation of a masterpiece, the impact of spiritual crisis on the evolution of a style, the imaginary portrait of the 'dying empire' and its gods, as well as all of the rich excitement of the physical world, of sea and desert, jungle and sky, or the sensuous beauty of human form—all are evoked with depth of insight and verbal splendour. These latter evocations remind us of certain contemporaries. The sensuality brings to mind the *Noces* of Camus which at one point confronts the evanescent life of the Midi with the stones of Florence. And in more austere moments, capturing the desert beyond Palmyra and the hostile spaces through which human art has made its way, we may think of the *Anabase* of St Jean Perse, with its fascination in the desert, its mélange of rigour and emptiness. These are Romantic images, and a Romantic sensibility will not be contained, even by imaginary walls.

When its serious contribution does not lie in a particular argument, but in the rich penumbra of impressionist criticism that surrounds it, the overt conflict within the Museum walls becomes itself eloquent testimony. We feel in all its anguish the tension between a doctrine which governs the right of Museum entry, and the presence of the vivid peripheral detail which testifies to the author's visual seduction by his subject matter. We may well understand the other conflict that lies behind it, that the nervous mouvementé adventurer is not entirely at ease in a funereal setting. However understood the original duality of Malraux remains and is unresolved. The heightened sense of life has also deepened the sense of shadow. No movement or colour or particular observation or personal enthusiasm or commitment has effaced that early impression of Drieu 'Le propre de son génie est de faire sentir d'abord la puissance d'absorption d'un moi solitaire. . . '[1] In the end the sense of isolation is profound enough to give both grandeur and pathos to the great rhetorician, wandering and talking alone in the silent Museum, surrounded by those images which testify to the fact of man without a key to his meaning. It is a picture in half-light, like Valéry's dialogue in the underworld, where the

[1] Drieu La Rochelle, op. cit. 'The true nature of his genius is to make felt above all the power of absorption of a solitary self.'

shades of Socrates and Phaedrus wander, no longer by the Ilissus, but by the river of Time. There as in the timeless Museum it is words that remain, and the argument moves like that of *Les Voix du Silence*, from act to idea, to immortality—as from act, to art, to museum pieces. Here the problems of man and creation, action and contemplation, have their genuine if shadowy existence.

Index